Praise for WorkforceRx

"Van Ton-Quinlivan has mastered workforce development from more perspectives than anyone in the field. She knows the differing interests of private industry, the public sector, higher education and the union movement, and has offered up ways to bridge those worlds to collectively bring a diversity of working people into good jobs."

—Andy Van Kleunen, CEO, National Skills Coalition

"This book is great storytelling and a master class in big design thinking. Well worth reading."

—Tammy Johns, CEO of Strategy & Talent, former SVP Innovation and Workforce Solutions of ManpowerGroup

"Creating an inclusive economy takes intentionality. This book outlines the levers every state and region have at their disposal to create economic opportunity and equitable recovery."

—Stuart Andreason, Assistant Vice President and Director of the Center for Workforce and Economic Opportunity, Federal Reserve Bank of Atlanta

"Van has rewritten the human capital theory and practice. The book offers a critical analysis and thoughtful proposition of the skills ecosystem that the new economy needs. Van calls for all stakeholders to develop a sustainable and inclusive skills ecosystem."

—Dr. Soon Joo Gog, Chief Skills Officer, SkillsFuture Singapore

"A revolutionary set of public-private partnership prescriptions for how to reignite the American Dream from a unique leader who has been on both sides of the education/employment divide. *WorkforceRx* should be compulsory reading for every elected official, college president, and CEO."

—Ryan Craig, Managing Director of Achieve Partners and author of
A New U: Faster + Cheaper Alternatives to College and
College Disrupted: The Great Unbundling of Higher Education

"Chock full of practical advice for business people who need to find and grow talent. The book pays keen attention to diversity, equity and inclusion and how companies don't need to go at it alone."

—Helen Rule, Board President of the International Women's Forum,
Chairman of Imatech Group of Companies, Australia

"Van Ton-Quinlivan is a leader, a storyteller, and a problem solver, all key to helping cure the ills of our outdated and outmoded workforce development systems. *WorkforceRx* offers a prescription for navigating the new world of work, where postsecondary credentials are a critical part of the treatment and where business leaders, educators, policymakers and the workers themselves must work together to build a healthier new ecosystem."

—Jamie Merisotis, President & CEO, Lumina Foundation

"Van Ton-Quinlivan has pioneered the path—and has now provided a guide-book—for bringing employers and educators together to develop the skilled and adaptable workforce that is required to close the income gap and enable resilient regional economies. These cross-sector partnerships—focused on improving outcomes and reducing disparities—should be a priority strategy for civic leaders committed to more inclusive prosperity."

—James Mayer, National Public Service Award recipient, former CEO of California
Forward and Executive Director of the Little Hoover Commission

"Van Ton-Quinlivan very effectively reframed how community colleges in California delivered on workforce programs while executive vice chancellor of the state system, reshaping not only how those institutions operated but also influencing K-12, workforce, economic development and other public agencies. She describes the behind-the-scenes work to materialize policy ideas into implementation—which is where many can fall short."

—Mike Kirst, Professor Emeritus of Education at Stanford University and the longest serving President of California's (K-12) State Board of Education

"For the big challenges facing our country posed by the striation of our economy, this book gives a win-win roadmap for workers and employers."

—Dave Regan, President, SEIU–United Healthcare Workers West

"Brilliant. How Van comes up with solutions in really tricky and complicated environments should be inspiring to everyone in an organizational leadership role. And her book illustrates solutions that are repeatable and transferable. These insights and proposals hold relevance across national borders and different education systems."

—Mary-Ann Bell, Corporate Director at COGECO, NAV Canada, SNC-Lavalin and IGOPP, former SVP and COO, Bell Aliant, Canada

"Van has a mastery of the intersection of higher education, workforce and public policy. She weaves those worlds together into *WorkforceRx* so that leaders of public systems and companies can adopt and adapt the playbooks for our needs."

—Totsie Memela Khambula, CEO, South African Social Security Agency, former CEO of the Women's Development Business Trust, South Africa

VAN TON-QUINLIVAN

Work
Force Rx

Agile and Inclusive Strategies for
Employers, Educators and Workers
in Unsettled Times

Connecting People with
the Right Skills for the Right Jobs

Master Catalyst Press | MasterCatalyst.org

Published by Master Catalyst Press
Davis, California
www.mastercatalyst.org

Master Catalyst Press supports the right of authors by valuing copyright. The purpose of copyright is to encourage the production of works by authors and artists.

The scanning, recording, uploading, and distribution of this book, in whole or in part, without permission is a theft of the author's intellectual property. If you would like permission to use the material from the book (other than for review purposes), please submit a request via www.mastercatalyst.org.

Most Master Catalyst Press books are available at special quantity discounts for bulk purchase for promotion, fundraising and educational needs. For details or for speaking engagement inquiries, visit www.mastercatalyst.org.

While the author has made every effort to provide accurate Internet addresses at the time of publication, neither the publisher nor the author assumes any responsibility for errors or for changes that occur after publication. The publisher and author are not responsible for websites (or their content) that are not under its ownership.

ISBN 978-1-7376275-0-0 (ebook), 978-1-7376275-1-7 (pbk.), 978-1-7376275-2-4 (hardback)

Library of Congress Control Number: 2021915568

Printed in the United States of America

Editing by Salwa Emerson
Cover design by Vanessa Mendozzi
Author photo by Beth Baugher

Contents

With love to David, Nicholas, and Ryan.
With gratitude to Kim Thu, Vien, Celeste and Skip.

Foreword

Since 2013, the Institute for the Future has been inviting groups of practical visionaries—innovators who through their work are building positive futures in different domains, from education to work, technology, civic media, social justice, and other arenas of civic life. We see these people as signals of the kind of futures we want to build and amplify.

Van Ton-Quinlivan has been a practical visionary her entire career. She is powerfully adept at anticipating change and offering up pragmatic workforce development actions and public policies that look around the bend. After her tenure as executive vice chancellor of the California Community Colleges system, which serves two million students in the state, Van came to the Institute as an executive-in-residence. Her curiosity led her to explore many signals of change the Institute was researching, from potential uses of virtual and augmented reality for immersive learning, to evolution of platform economies and their impact on work arrangements and access to key assets for economic security, to alternative equitable business models.

Van took the opportunity to learn and connect trends in these different areas to create Futuro Health, a revolutionary new nonprofit whose aim is to fill the growing need for healthcare workers and that combines cooperative worker arrangements and agile educational solutions. As the CEO of Futuro Health, once again she is proving herself to be a risk taker and a master catalyst who can set into motion countless transformations in the private, public, and now nonprofit sectors.

In her book, Van illuminates many ways in which we can infuse agility into workforce and talent development. Her strategy playbooks remind us that it is up to us to design the human infrastructure we need to thrive in the future ahead. In this she exemplifies the Institute for the Future mantra: the purpose of futures thinking is not to predict the future but to systematically think about future possibilities and engage in actions that help build a desirable future.

We are not passive bystanders to the future; the future is not something that just happens to us; we have agency to build the kind of future we want to live in. Rather than fretting about robots taking away jobs, Van shows us how our long-standing institutions of higher education and an ecosystem approach can cultivate an inclusive and skilled workforce for the future.

Marina Gorbis

Executive Director, Institute for the Future

Introduction

For my first job out of Stanford Business School, I was hired into a management training program at a major telecommunications firm in California. Just two years into my tenure, the firm announced its merger with a Texas-based utility company. Despite the external façade of a friendly nuptial, it was not a merger of equals. The other company eventually took over all decision-making and restructuring, including the firing of dozens of longtime employees who held leadership roles. *Duplicative* was the word of the hour. Practically overnight, the leaders who oversaw my management program—chief financial officers, vice presidents, senior directors, and directors—lost their job security. The merger needed to drive out cost.

The disruption wiped clean the new company's whiteboard, so to speak. These devoted employees had invested years of their lives into the company, becoming experts at navigating its corridors, and storing away chits of goodwill to use as barter at a later date.

As a newbie, I was caught off-guard when senior leaders who had been at the company for years started seeking my advice about transitioning their careers. They'd known how to play the game internally, building up relationship equity and stacking the chips to ensure their ascension up the corporate ladder. However, when it came to accessing mobility across their industry, they found themselves in unfamiliar territory. Some had not sought an external job for over a decade. And the longer their tenure, the more they worried about their ability to find a new employer.

The situation was disorienting. I came into the company with many assumptions about the formula for success, yet going through a merger, I learned important ways to navigate disruptions, look ahead, and future-proof.

Interestingly, the sense of vulnerability pervasive during the time of the merger felt hauntingly familiar. It was not my first experience with a blank slate. I was a child of war. My family escaped to the US as refugees from Vietnam, so I already knew firsthand what it was like to suddenly find yourself in unknown territory with little guidance, to question whether your assumptions still applied to the current day, to redefine yourself for the changed context, and to embrace risk inherent in picking the future you want.

In our current global economic crisis, most of us can empathize with these experiences. As an immigrant, I know that these life lessons lie at the heart of my own story.

Falling Back on Education

"Your mother and I will not give you kids lots of material things," my father would tell us when we were growing up. "Stuff can be taken away." My father grew up an orphan, despite being born into a well-to-do family. His parents died prematurely during a domestic unrest akin to China's Cultural Revolution. Once again in 1975, he would lose everything. "Instead, we're giving you an education. That can never be taken away." To this day, my father's words still echo in my ears, for I took to heart this value that he passed on to me.

In Vietnam, our family led an upper-middle-class life. My father was a neurosurgeon, and my mother a teacher, one of the most highly respected occupations in Asian culture. When the war broke out, everything changed. Status and wealth no longer guaranteed people's ability to thrive. Suddenly, we were among everyone else whose lives and livelihoods were disrupted. My father was fortunately sent on a fellowship to study at a military hospital in Hawaii. There, he worked until he could send for my mother, my two sisters, and me.

I was six years old when we boarded an evacuation helicopter, each of us girls carrying in our tiny grips a small Pan Am shoulder bag that contained one outfit, one rice ball, and a can of condensed milk—provisions in case we got separated from each other. It was early April 1975, just before the official fall of Vietnam. Thanks to a string of connections and miraculously sequenced events, we managed to get out in the nick of time.

My family would be telling a very different story today if it were not for the generosity of many who helped in our escape and eventual resettlement in the United States. We were lucky enough to land in Hawaii whose history and infrastructure was well built to support high volumes of immigrants, since, historically, Hawaii had imported Japanese laborers to work the sugarcane fields.

Upon landing on the island of Oahu, we stayed temporarily with a generous sponsor, Dr. Eugene George, an American military doctor who would later go on to serve US presidents, and his wife.

Our family eventually found housing. My sisters and I grew up on free lunch tokens, community dental work, English-as-a-second-language lessons, and food stamps. My brother, who was born many years later, would experience a very different upbringing. I thrived in school and graduated from Henry J. Kaiser High School as class president and salutatorian. I had no clue about choosing a career; I just knew I wanted to go to college because, as my parents had taught us, education was what we could fall back on in the end.

Georgetown University in Washington, DC, seemed the ideal college to broaden my understanding of the world, given the campus's proximity to the nation's capital. My application was accepted, and while I earned my degree there, I learned to appreciate the partnership of government entities, a concept that permeated my academics and activities. Years later, this nascent understanding of public systems would resurface and come to my aid when my company faced workforce challenges.

The Strong Workforce Playbook

If you're reading this book, chances are you are looking for a new perspective on the problems of work and workers and the solutions offered by workforce development. Whether you are an employer, a government policy maker, an educator, or an involved citizen, you may sense that the answers are not so far away. And you're right.

I define workforce development as proactive tactics that equip an organization with the right people with the right skills at the right time. This book concentrates on skill gaps and worker shortages at the entry-level, midskill, and even high-skill functions, including engineering occupations. In short, when a company or organization realizes that it cannot readily find the skillsets it needs, that's when workforce development comes into play.

HR practices, like succession planning for a company's managerial leadership positions and the development of high potentials, which are distinct, are not the domain of this book. Minimally, workforce development addresses operational pain points when it comes to hiring and retention. When done well, it also creates a win-win situation of economic and social mobility for the local community surrounding the employer. Exemplary workforce development breaks out of the mold of assuming every organization must solve the issue on its own and engages collaboratively with employers (who are peers or competitors), education, government, labor unions, and/or community-based organizations to form an ecosystem of the willing.

Agile, by definition, is the ability to move quickly and easily. An ecosystem of willing partners within a workforce ecosystem can provide agility during unsettled times by pivoting with changing trends and shifting conditions while still delivering to employers the right people with the right skills at the right time.

In my application essay for business school, I stated that I wanted to learn the tools of the private sector to make a difference in education. I wasn't sure yet exactly what that meant, but I knew that finding out was a vital part of my professional journey and a way to pay forward opportunity to others. I was attracted to Stanford by a program called the Public Management Initiative, which bridged the gap between the private and public sectors. Each year, business school students proposed and voted to adopt one concept. In my year, I proposed a joint venture between the business school and education school entitled Partnerships for Business and Education (P4E).

I led this winning initiative with the belief that for every problem that presents itself in the education system, a solution (or derivative thereof) already exists somewhere else. We need to find and adapt it to our local need. It's easy be lured into thinking each dilemma is novel when we're engaging with education from the seat of a corporation or as an elected official, community member, parent, or citizen. In truth, the first step to finding a solution is to peel the layers off the onion to understand the intricacies of each challenge. The second step is to find an applicable playbook for addressing the challenge.

This book is a compilation of workforce development solutions I have successfully employed and contoured throughout the years. As you will see, I came to tackle more and more complex challenges in workforce development over time as the stakeholders and my span of responsibilities grew. Regardless of whether my paycheck came from the energy or healthcare industry, from the private, public, or nonprofit sectors, I found that the plays in this book still apply.

I've come to learn these proven solutions through experimentation and adaptation. I studied models and practices and applied their lessons to new situations to see whether doing so would bear fruit. Initially, I practiced these principles of workforce development in the private sector while at Pacific Gas and Electric (PG&E). When Governor Jerry Brown subsequently appointed me to head the workforce mission of the California Community Colleges, the largest system of higher education in the nation with now 116 institutions serving more than two million students, I shifted from the private to the public sector. This was my opportunity to pay it forward.

As vice chancellor and then executive vice chancellor, I put in place a set of changes under the banner of *Doing What MATTERS for Jobs and the Economy* that led to unprecedented expansion and innovation of career education in the system. The principles became incorporated into legislation called the Strong Workforce Program. Other states would eventually seek to borrow the playbook for their own needs, just as California learned from others. The passage of the Workforce Innovation and Opportunity Act (WIOA) codified a number of practices into federal policy.

Truly effective problem solving involves the use of a four-letter word most elected and appointed policy makers, government agency administrators, and institutional stakeholders try to avoid. It involves *risk*. I amassed these lessons because I was in the position to take the risk to learn.

Risk: The Only Way to Survive

As I was growing up, my parents were too busy trying to survive in a new country to hover over me the way parents, myself included, tend to do nowadays. My sisters and I were left to manage for ourselves when we were young. We took care of each other, did our own schoolwork, solved our own problems, and sneaked in more than a bit of television before our parents came home.

My parents struggled to have the family land on its feet. My father redid his medical residency from scratch as was required to work as a physician in the US. My mother took up bookkeeping to pay the bills. While the restart was humbling, my parents never expressed regret or bitterness for our situation. They were always grateful that our family had a chance for a better life. Because they were too busy orienting to a new land with new norms, neither parent put undue pressure on us to live up to any expectation other than to study. This gave us the freedom to risk. And when I tried something new, I found new possibilities. I came to realize that my own opportunities were limited more by my mental construct and internal voice of judgment than reality.

We adults usually learn by doing. I learned my most thought-provoking lessons in workforce development by taking risks. I gave up a good job to take on a riskier one in order to advocate for different approaches on how to build talent, which resulted in the PowerPathway workforce development program at Pacific Gas and Electric (PG&E). I advanced policies and practices that challenged the long-standing status quo. As vice chancellor, I changed the terms for grant funding to bring colleges into regional collaboration instead of continuing to compete with each other. I sought and built ecosystems of the willing—eventually converging a diverse set of stakeholders to serve on the Board of Governors Task Force on Jobs, Economy, and a Strong Workforce (abbreviated as the Strong Workforce Task Force).

The task force crafted twenty-five recommendations for how to expand career education in the state, which later were adopted into regulation and legislation. I took the arrows for advancing changes, in the hope of giving students opportunities that weren't so readily available, the way others had done for me. In doing so, I came to discover and understand possibilities for workforce development practices and policies that would never have revealed themselves otherwise.

Rethinking Education to Future-Proof the Workforce

Without a doubt, education is a common denominator and necessary ingredient in the competitiveness of industries and organizations. The role of higher education continually comes up when I'm a part of discussions, whether led by the National Governors Association, National Council on Competitiveness, National Commission on Energy Policy, National Advisory Committee on Apprenticeship, or President's Economic Recovery Advisory Board Education and Training Subcommittee. I wrote this book because I believe wholeheartedly in higher education's indispensability and pertinence to the future of the workforce.

When I finished graduate school with dual master's degrees in business and education policy, I worked first at a large telecommunications utility for a few years, then at an internet infrastructure start-up, followed by an education technology company.

Throughout those years, during my downtime, I found myself reading up on education policy articles to relax. A faculty friend, knowing my dilettante interest in education, invited me to teach a class at a community college in California. In an eye-opening moment, I entered the classroom, looked around at the diverse student body, and thought, This is where the workforce of the state will come from. I was struck.

During the entire time I studied education policy at Stanford, no one had ever spoken about the health of community colleges, which apparently were the unrecognized stepchildren of higher education. True to my own method of problem solving, I started to peel back the layers, embarking on a learning journey that would take me to the issue's core. I researched, talked to policy experts, volunteered, and followed the money flow until I started to find answers.

Then one day, my former boss from the telecommunications company, who had now become CEO of the larger energy utility, (PG&E), called to ask me to work for him as his special assistant. Between the births of my two sons, I'd been out of the work world for more than four years, a decision that for most women in corporate is a career-stalling move. Now, I was being invited to reenter and work with the C-suite level, which was a rare opportunity I couldn't overlook. Even more appealing was the unique vantage point I'd have to explore my developing passion for workforce development. Although I'd already just enrolled in a doctoral program, I couldn't resist the invitation to put in motion, firsthand, some of the principles I'd already been learning about. I accepted the position.

The Diversity-versus-Quality Myth

In my new role at PG&E, I gained access to the entire company. All doors were open. I took advantage of that access to speak with supervisors to learn their pain points when it came to hiring talent and retaining a workforce.

From the voices of those leading the operations, I heard their reluctance to do workforce development because they felt pressured by Government Relations to take on diverse hires who were insufficiently screened and mostly ended up poor performers who needed to be managed out. These positions in PG&E's field operations required more than a high school degree but less than a bachelor's degree, hence, not a match for the traditional four-year college recruiting channels. The HR department explained it was nearly impossible to find quality together with diversity, no matter how much the company tried working with community-based partners to do outreach.

Applicants sourced by local community organizations were diverse but underskilled; at most, only one out of thirty could pass the written test even before undergoing the drug test and background check.

Frankly, the complaint about diversity at the expense of quality infuriated me. As an immigrant, I knew that many of the well-paid jobs at the company would be the ultimate dream come true for many workers from underserved communities who had devoted their lives to vocational success. I began speaking with the operations supervisors at PG&E to get to the root of the problem and came up with a one-page plan that required only a small pledge of money and support.

The concept was to leverage the public infrastructure and tap into the natural feeder pool of the community college system locally available everywhere. I knew we could reliably have diversity and quality, but we had to go about it in a very different way. I named the strategy PG&E PowerPathway. Within roughly two and a half years, this initiative catapulted to the stage as a nationally recognized industry best practice.

The Win-Win Plan

I pitched my one-page plan to the CEO Peter Darbee, the chief HR officer John Simon, and the head of philanthropy Ophelia Basgal, explaining to them that a well-executed offensive strategy to improve PG&E's standing with underserved communities and social justice groups (similar to but much earlier than Black Lives Matter) was a win-win for the company's reputation in addition to meeting the staffing needs of the operations. They agreed to give me the opportunity to demonstrate the new model of workforce development.

From a role as the right hand of the CEO, occupying a twenty-ninth-floor office that overlooked the Bay Bridge, engaging in the highest level strategic discussions of the entire company, I transitioned to a dungeon of an office on the second floor with no amenities to speak of. I'd given up the status of the twenty-ninth executive floor to become a back-office function. If the one-page plan didn't work, I'd be stuck on the floor indefinitely. It was a high-risk career step.

Then I remembered what Bettie Steiger, one of my lifelong mentors and an early Silicon Valley female executive, had taught me about the transformative power of taking risks: "You need to give up who you are in order to become who you can be." Her words are a continual reminder of where I came from as a refugee. I started from a ground leveled by war and, through education, repeatedly reinvented myself to align my life and career with my values—always with the idea of helping others and paying forward opportunity.

I wanted everyone to be able to begin the race at the same starting line and had decided to devote my later life's work to fixing the systemic problems evident in the intersection of higher education and workforce that keep people from doing so. I decided to take the risk and continue with my purpose.

Tapping into the Power of Community Colleges

Policy makers and employers had started looking to education to address the *skills gap*, which was the term used to describe the imbalance between supply and demand of talent. The country was starting to tap into the power of community colleges to match the right talent with the right jobs.

In 2009, the newly elected Obama administration began advocating that everyone should have the opportunity to have one year of college under their belt in order to access the middle class. That year, I helped announce the White House Skills for America's Future initiative, which was designed to improve industry partnerships with community colleges and build a nationwide network to maximize workforce development, job training, and job placement.

Paired with that event was the first White House Community College Summit, hosted by Dr. Jill Biden, where out of more than one hundred guests, I was among the handful of corporate leaders in attendance.

In 2011, I was appointed Vice Chancellor of Workforce and Economic Development for California's Community Colleges, a position that allowed me the budget and scope to put into practice the collective wisdom I'd accrued over the years. I eventually took responsibility for the system's technology portfolio when promoted to Executive Vice Chancellor of Workforce and Digital Futures.

During my eight-year tenure as an appointee of Governor Jerry

Brown, my team and I grew public investment to expand workforce programs from $100 million to more than $1 billion. We redesigned the tools of public policy pertinent to the state's delivery of career education, apprenticeship, and adult education—and did so by reshaping monies, metrics, and data. We created the conditions for innovation by getting diverse stakeholders—employers, educators, government policy makers, labor, and community leaders—on board.

Growing with the Gig

Even before the pandemic, the rules of the future of work were already changing, a process largely driven by the growing size of the gig economy where millions of freelance, independent, and platform-based workers sought work and not full-time employment.

You and I found this new economy convenient as we used Uber, GrubHub, TaskRabbit, and other new consumer options. But then I learned from Wingham Rowan who spoke at the California Economic Summit about the plight of the "irregular workers" who could only make money by pasting together multiple gigs one day at a time. These workers, including the likes of home health aides, would be informed by employers day-by-day what their schedules would be if they were to work at all.

I wondered how workers with young children managed childcare when working this type of on-call schedule. Rowan challenged us to think up solutions on how to preserve the opportunity but correct the tenuous status faced by this underclass of gig workers. It occurred to me then that we had not yet adapted the human infrastructure to pair with the next economy.

Then COVID-19 came. The pandemic hit Americans hard, including gig workers. Once again, the context changed, this time for millions. Those who lost their livelihood found themselves precluded from accessing unemployment benefits because they were not recognized by law as eligible. Again, the human infrastructure lagged and needed to be continually adapted to create new models that suit work and workers. Collective ingenuity across the private, nonprofit, government, labor, and education sectors would help peel back the layers of issues, take risk to experiment, and adapt the plays in the workforce development book for the future of work.

The following chapters address specific workforce challenges and their proven solutions, with the exception of the last chapter, which discusses the latest issues unique to the post-pandemic gig economy and is merely a start to finding answers. As a collective whole, this book is a testimony to the vast scope of what is possible when we create and maintain an agile workforce. My hope is that by reading it you will not only glimpse firsthand the power behind smart collaboration, but also become an active participant in the conversation.

First, let's start with how corporations, policy makers, and educators can aggregate the demand for labor to match the right people with the right jobs.

One

Making the Fire Hose and the
Garden Hose Work Together

CHALLENGE:

How do you match
the right people with the right skills
at the right time?

SOLUTION:

Corporations, education institutions,
and public policy makers must
aggregate the demand for labor and
collaborate on curricula.

In the corporate world, one of the most ubiquitous complaints bewildering business leaders is this: Why doesn't the education system produce what I need? Until the last decade or so, higher education had its own well-established academic processes distinctly siloed from those of employers. Shaping curricula and what students learned, for example, remained the protected domain of educators, who generally resisted the input of industry.

I remember when, in my PG&E role as Director of Workforce Development, my initial approach with Fresno City College to create a workforce development program was met with skepticism. I could hear the questioning tone of the college administrators, Why should we trust this corporation?

Conversely, employers had their established playbook for securing entry-level and midlevel technical workers: job boards, employee referrals, headhunters, and college campus recruitment. Historically, this playbook did not include strategies to intentionally leverage the public higher education infrastructure as a talent feeder in ways beyond the occasional job posting in the career center.

The divide of the two worlds became obvious when it came time to look at student employability. In June 2020, CEO Maria Flynn of the national nonprofit Jobs for the Future wrote, "Less than a quarter of employers believe graduates are prepared to start a career after college, and only one-quarter of working Americans who attended college strongly believe their education is relevant to their work."

And in a survey of employers and college students conducted on behalf of the Association of American Colleges & Universities, employers consistently gave college graduates a low score for preparedness among seventeen work-relevant skills, while students thought themselves better prepared than they actually were.

The world of work was already changing with foreseeable automation, digitization, machine learning, and other impacts on a large swath of the workforce. These signals were not limited to the blue-collar workforce, as they had been in the past. Parties ranging from the World Economic Forum, to management consulting firm McKinsey & Company, and the National Skills Coalition convened discussions on how best to navigate the looming future. Signature initiatives, research reports, and books on the future of work proliferated.

Multiple governors convened their task forces on the future of work to ponder the implications, including California's Commission on the Future of Work. The National Governors Association conducted roundtables nationwide on Future Workforce Now to generate policy recommendations.

The COVID-19 pandemic in 2020 jarringly altered the terrain of work, further widening the chasm between employment demands and job readiness. A McKinsey & Company study of executives in 800 companies across the globe concluded, "Since the start of COVID-19, executives say adoption of digitization and automation technologies has accelerated." While the report notes that automation intensified, "including robotics, autonomous vehicles, and AI-driven software that can perform processing workflows," the rate of automation was not as fast as that of digitization, a difference that placed undue pressure on employees to upgrade technological skills at unprecedented rates.

To make matters worse, the demographics of students now pursuing higher education have gotten more complicated. Before the pandemic, the population of traditional-age students—that is, the youths feeding into the college system directly from high schools—was projected to drop by roughly 15% between 2025 and 2030, according to the Strada Education Network. The pandemic likely hastened that projected shrinkage by driving down overall postsecondary and secondary school attendance.

Finally, with the younger generation on the numerical decline, and the large population of baby boomers moving into retirement, we're shifting from a pyramid-shaped talent pool to one that is more cylindrical in nature. Couple this fact with the reduction in work visas for foreign workers under the Trump administration and diminished enrollment of foreign students in US colleges, and we are facing a different pool of onshore, skilled talent than in the past.

It is up to us to act with intention to create the workforce with the right skills at the right time. The alternative is what some call "post and pray," which is the act of posting job opportunities without knowing if there is a talent pool to fill it.

If we are to build a talent pool, there is something important to consider and understand: What makes higher education institutions tick? Colleges rely on enrollment to keep programs running. And enrollment is a factor that is normally entirely out of the hands of industry. Yet, a talent shortage like the one we are facing now requires tailored and creative solutions—the kind of solutions that my experience in the industry has taught me how to find.

The Pool versus the Puddle

I mentioned my humble beginnings as a refugee from the Vietnam War. My family and I immigrated to the United States with not much more than a single carry-on piece of luggage on each person when we were evacuated from the country. I was six. It didn't matter that my father had been a neurosurgeon in Vietnam or that my mother had been a teacher. Once in the United States, we were like every other refugee who came to a new land. Our common task was learning a new culture.

How did I go from being a kid who spoke no English to becoming a high school salutatorian and class president? Many factors came into play, some I'll never even know. But I do know that I observed and listened keenly to pick up the cues around me—how to phrase my words, how to dress to fit in, what foods my fellow classmates liked to eat. The journey was filled with trial and error and, often, embarrassment. But what was the alternative?

That same ability to observe and listen followed me into adulthood. When I became the Director of Workforce Development at PG&E, a company of nearly 20,000 employees, I had a knack for hearing pain when it arose. Pain served as my cue. PG&E provided electricity and gas to a large swath of the state. I sought out conversations with the company's operations supervisors and division heads, always asking them whether or not they had the workforce they wanted when they needed it. Some did. Some didn't.

Periodically, I would find someone for whom the problem was acute enough to keep them up at night. These supervisors were responsible for big technical operations that relied on classifications of employees like systems operators, line workers, gas technicians, utility workers, welders, mechanics, and customer service representatives who staffed the phone banks. Supervisors of smaller divisions, whose staff had titles like energy efficiency engineers, also expressed frustration when trying to hire from the apparent talent puddle.

I probed for the intensity of their pain and asked a series of questions to peel back the layers. When did the problem begin? Was it getting worse? How long was the need expected to last? What was the volume of hiring per year? Supervisors talked openly about their efforts and frustrations to find the skillsets they needed. Others wanted to find qualified candidates from a diverse pool to ensure their workforce reflected the communities being served, yet they were stymied by the deficit of skills.

In short, they were finding it nearly impossible to find the right people with the right skills at the right time to staff their operations. Their concerns, it turned out, were pervasive across the aging energy, gas, and nuclear industries, which at that time faced a nationwide demographics challenge whereby 25 to 50% of the workforce became retirement eligible within ten years, according to the Center for Energy Workforce Development.

By listening to these supervisors' stories, I used cues in the conversations to determine how ready they were to find solutions through workforce development. After all, doing so required their time and resources, though mostly time. As a rule of thumb, when the volume of hiring is countable on one or two hands, I find it better to transact for talent through traditional methods like job postings, employee referral programs, or using a recruiter.

However, when an organization starts using fingers and toes to count the number of openings, and they lack confidence in the hiring process—essentially, they are doing the equivalent of "post and pray"—it's time to attempt new approaches offered by workforce development. Of course, doing so is an endeavor that takes longer than the quarter-by-quarter horizon of most corporations. But engaging in workforce development could significantly deepen the shallow talent pool for the long term.

Moving the Fleet

As one of the largest gas and electric companies in the country, PG&E has an enormous fleet of vehicles to match its size, including cars, trucks, hydraulic cranes, snowplows, and more. The company was also located in California, a state where public policies highly valued green energy, and regulators wanted to lead the way in energy efficiency. PG&E aggressively adopted electric vehicle technology to further the public-policy agenda to be green and reduce greenhouse gas emissions since traditional vehicles powered by combustion engines were high polluters.

In 2009, I got to sit down with Dave Meisel, an unassuming man who wore wire-framed glasses, who led PG&E's massive fleet consisting of over 15,000 pieces of equipment. I listened to his workforce needs. Dave had more than thirty-two years of experience in the transportation industry including fleet operations, logistics, and distribution and was facing a serious numbers dilemma. He was the purchaser of the largest fleet of electric vehicles to date and was ingesting the vehicles faster than the manufacturer could train his crew to service them. If his mechanics attempted maintenance of one of the electric vehicles before getting certified through the manufacturer's training, the warranty on that vehicle would automatically be void. The manufacturer was shipping vehicles more quickly than it had the capacity to train its mechanics. This operational issue kept Dave up at night.

The timing couldn't have been worse since not only were his mechanics untrained in the new electric vehicle technology, but his entire maintenance staff mirrored the industry's aging demographics. Dave's fleet workforce was 325 mechanics. His sleep was also troubled as he worried about how to backfill the difficult-to-replace senior mechanics who were at risk of retiring. No one had submitted their paperwork yet, but Dave knew the time was on the horizon.

In an interview in *Fleet Management Weekly*, he listed workforce as his second top challenge: "Our incredibly talented, but senior, workforce will reach retirement age in the next couple of years. That is an especially large challenge for us. Recruiting quality people has never been a problem for our company, but it is very difficult to replace the historical knowledge that leaves when our senior people retire." Surely, the interview struck a major chord throughout the industry.

Dave's first problem was that the vehicles were coming in at a rate outpacing the manufacturer's capacity to certify PG&E's mechanics. As I listened to him talk about his concerns, my spider sense started to tingle. I knew that the solution existed somewhere, perhaps close by but still beyond the walls of PG&E.

I searched the community colleges in PG&E's footprint and found a network of eight with automotive programs whose instructors' knowledge was close enough to the expertise we needed to handle the new fleet technology. I started to court this group and found seven instructors willing to be trained by Dave's master mechanic in electric vehicle maintenance. The manufacturer made an exception to allow PG&E's master mechanic to train these seven faculty members, who would in turn train Dave's mechanics.

Logistically, this was no small feat. PG&E's mechanics were situated across a massive span of geography, from Bakersfield on the central, far west side of California all the way up to its northern border with Oregon, covering more than half the state. Subsequently, those seven community college instructors trained more than 325 mechanics at PG&E. These training sessions often had to take place at odd times since mechanics operated on eight-hour, round-the-clock shifts. Despite the odds, we managed to solve the operational problem using this novel workforce development playbook.

It was invigorating to watch the public sector help the private sector and, in turn, expand the capacity of the community colleges to perpetuate the skills in future graduates. Beyond resolving Dave's immediate operational problem, this collaboration between a corporation and an educational institution yielded an even more profound benefit. Those seven colleges whose instructors had rolled up their sleeves and dove in had, in the process, learned new technology and subsequently upgraded their curricula into their regular classrooms. By incorporating the latest electric vehicle competencies, they increased the day-one readiness of their students.

Dave Meisel became very supportive of leveraging the public infrastructure to solve workforce problems after that point. He eventually served on the statewide advisory board that formed when I became appointed Vice Chancellor of Workforce and Economic Development of the California Community Colleges, the largest system of higher education in the nation with then 113 institutions. Dave came to understand firsthand the benefits of private-public collaboration.

Closing the Gap

Dave had a second problem: the aging out of the most senior tier of his mechanics in his workforce, with no strategy for how to replace them. He knew replacements could not be easily recruited. The talent pool was shallow for the specialized skills that PG&E needed. The solution lay in a different playbook. This time, to create the hires he needed, I decided to use a scalpel approach since he was looking at possible attrition rates of roughly three to five senior mechanics per year over the next five years.

Again, the solution lay in leveraging the public infrastructure. This time, we sourced the one community college whose curriculum matched closest to the skills we needed. We offered PG&E's master mechanic a chance to work side-by-side with the instructor and design a compressed course with the necessary curriculum to bridge the gap.

We sent thirty of our own people to the three-month program. Five became "ready now" and were put onto the list as possible replacements for when a master mechanic retired. And since Dave only needed five replacements a year, the remaining trainees were given feedback and had time to plug the holes in their knowledge and experience.

Pooling Jobs

Through solving Dave's and other supervisors' hiring problems, I observed a key friction point that hinders education and employers from collaborating more readily. I call it the fire hose versus the garden hose dilemma. Fundamentally, employers drip out jobs like a garden hose, with one, two, or three of the same jobs at most posted at a time.

At the same time, education needs to have sufficient enrollees, more than just a trickle, to make it financially prudent for the college to hold a class. Usually, this number is twenty-five but no less than fifteen for nonlecture programs. Below this volume, we couldn't get the interest of a college to make the special effort to update curricula for the latest industry skillsets. This type of mismatch creates timing issues for when students are ready to seek work and when employers post their jobs. Ideally, we need a solution that combines the agility of a garden hose with the power and water pressure of a fire hose.

How did we solve this dilemma with what we had under our control? A simple strategy was to batch up our job postings of the same or similar occupations and time their posting with when classes completed and students were ready to find jobs. The second strategy involved talking to companies in our supply chain, like the vendors who performed industrial tree trimming services for PG&E, to see if they were willing to hire alongside us. Third, we engaged our competitors who hired similar classifications.

The hiring consortium adopted a strategy of collaborating first to create the talent pool then competing later when it came time to hire. At first, it didn't feel natural to collaborate with competitors.

But the alternative to collaboration would be to "post and pray" or poach from each other in the shallow talent puddle, options that were no longer working.

Flexing within Curricula

I uncovered another solution for my workforce development playbook when an interesting issue arose as we tried to pool jobs to obtain more than twenty-five of them. By batching three occupations, we aggregated the needed volume. However, while the three shared much in common, they also had differences. None of the occupations was sufficient in volume to have its own course. We wrestled with what to do.

My program manager, Keith Lovgren, and the faculty at Fresno City College came up with a novel curricular design comprised of a common curriculum and swing weeks. To acknowledge what we had in common, all twenty-five students were enrolled in a three-month PG&E PowerPathway training program to become utility workers. But, to increase their marketability and competitiveness for the specific roles that we anticipated at the end of the program, the third month of training consisted of two swing weeks of learning that digressed from the common curriculum and specialized in one of the three occupations.

Five of the students, for instance, learned about the systems operator roles since there were five vacancies. Ten learned about gas utility worker occupations. The remaining ten prepped for the electric worker role, thus dividing up the cohort to be ready for specific jobs available. To instruct during the swing weeks, we recruited retirees and company employees.

Upskilling When Technology Shifts

In 2019, after my tenure as executive vice chancellor with the California Community Colleges, I became an Executive-in-Residence with the Institute for the Future, headquartered near Stanford University. In that capacity, I spoke to a group of a dozen chief human resources officers (CHRO) in Silicon Valley. I sat in on their roundtable, where each shared an operational dilemma with which they were wrestling.

One CHRO talked about how his company was shifting to a cloud-based strategy, a move that made him anxious because he would have to fire their current engineers and replace them with cloud engineers. The problem, he explained, was a lack of cloud engineers in the market to fill those positions. To hire new talent, the company would have to pay top dollar, especially since his company did not have the hot tech company allure of others and the shortage was very acute for this skillset.

As the CHRO spoke, my spider sense kicked in once again. Why not work with a willing higher education partner to develop a course that closed the gap between what his engineers knew and the needed cloud computing skillsets demanded by the technology shift? He could offer the training to his incumbent engineers. Those employees uninterested in the training would decline and exit. But many would opt in.

The CHRO had never considered this playbook to upskill his employees and expressed great relief at finding a different option than "post and pray." Better yet, just as in the prior example where the community college faculty who trained the mechanics brought their newfound knowledge back into their regular classrooms, the same would occur in this instance, with the college folding cloud computing skills into its regular programming—better preparing future students and deepening the talent puddle into a pool. Again, a win-win.

The Three-Legged Stool

The goal of workforce development is to reliably produce the workforce with the right skills at the right time. I find it helpful to think about the foundation of workforce development as a three-legged stool of collaboration, when each party does not do everything but merely focuses on what it does best. The first leg is the employers, whose role is to articulate their hiring requirements and then eventually hire. The second leg is an entity rooted in the community who can conduct outreach, screening, and case management, always keeping diversity and employer qualifications in mind. The third leg is the education provider, whose expertise can provide the right training to close the gap between where candidates are and what employers request.

I have already spoken at length about the first leg in my examples with PG&E acting in private-public collaboration, where the employer's role is to articulate their hiring requirements and then eventually hire.

One piece of advice I'd like to give to employers, in their role as the first leg, is to have an understanding of their own internal process for hiring from beginning to end. Viable candidates for PG&E, for example, could only be those over eighteen years in age, who pass the drug test, have no felony on the background check, are in possession of a class A driver's license, and can pass a suite of company-specific pre-employment batteries. These were nonnegotiable hiring requirements of the company.

For certain occupations such as line workers, the ones who come to fix your downed power line, there were additional predictors of suitability. For example, candidates can't be afraid of heights. PG&E's ability to be clear about our minimum and preferred qualifications spurred our partners (who served as the second leg of the stool) to design into the screening process an exercise where candidates climbed up and down a very tall ladder to show their aptitude to work at heights. Our partners also screened out all candidates who could not meet our minimum qualifications.

Let me spend a moment on the second leg, whose function is to conduct outreach, screening, and case management. The second leg can be a community-based organization or public agency partner as long as they can generate and case manage a diverse talent pool to enter into and persist through the workforce development program. It may seem overly obvious, but one principle I find myself repeating is this: If you want diversity to be in the talent pool, then the beginning of the workforce development pipeline needs to be diverse. This means that outreach for diversity has to be done early. Public workforce agencies and community-based organizations can do a better job going deeper and wider into communities to bring awareness of the jobs than what most companies have the appetite to do.

I remember Pat Barr, the case manager from the Fresno Regional Workforce Development Board who was assigned to partner with my company. She was a no-nonsense retired school principal. I was impressed by her effort to generate high-quality, diverse candidates for my company's PowerPathway training program.

She interviewed applicants in ways accessible and comfortable to candidates, including meeting up at the food court in the shopping mall instead of at her out-of-the-way office. She asked the hard questions to ascertain their motivations and put candidates through the drug tests and background checks to ensure their eligibility.

For each class, she gave us a full roster of diverse candidates, along with five alternates. She and her boss, Blake Konzcal, taught me the value of using the ACT WorkKeys® assessments as a standardized way to determine baseline numeracy and literacy specific to an occupation. Using this common tool left less to interpretation during the screening process. And employers indexed the WorkKeys score to the actual ability requirements of the occupation. I saw our workforce development program completion rates skyrocket, thanks to Pat's use of this tool. Having learned this lesson, I subsequently requested that all our partners administer the same tool moving forward.

Key to the third leg, finding the education provider with expertise to do the training, is locating a willing and capable partner, which may not be the most visible or nearest institution to you. Employers need to cast a net more broadly for an education partner with the desired competencies, capacity, and interest. Admittedly, the stars sometimes don't align. If a college has a willing administrator but the involved faculty have no bandwidth, then the partnership will not yield fruit.

Fortunately, in this modern day when online modalities are becoming more commonplace, there is more choice. I was fascinated by how Fresno City College masterminded the curriculum to close the gap on the skills needed by my company. The three-month course designed by their faculty included electricity as well as energy industry fundamentals, skills relevant to passing the company's pre-employment test, and a physical regimen to get every adult into shape.

PG&E's pre-employment batteries had some topics where candidates predictably struggled. Some adults felt challenged by spatial reasoning, for example, so the faculty incorporated a workbook to practice visualizing blocks graphed on paper, rotated in different arrangements. Students struggled with timed test-taking, for most had not done so in over a decade, so the faculty created drills to give them practice, the same way high school students would prep to take the SAT or ACT standardized exams.

Our company also needed candidates to be in good physical shape. Three days a week, the students, of whom many were military veterans, would play soccer games to ready their physique for the physical portion of the pre-employment test.

You may wonder whether it is fair to prepare candidates in this way. The reality was that the company's traditional applicant pipeline had friends and family within the company to give them tips on how best to prepare. Those from underserved communities were not privy to these details and thus came unprepared. Inviting diversity means leveling the playing field of how people prepare. In chapter 7, I will rediscuss the three-legged stool and its aim to level the playing field relative to the concepts of diversity, equity, and inclusion (DEI).

CHAPTER HIGHLIGHTS

- More and more, the education system that we have does not produce what employers need from workers.
- The worlds of education and employment can no longer afford to operate in silos, disconnected from each other's respective priorities.
- This gulf is accelerating as developments in modern technology are changing the world of work at a rapid pace.
- This is a time-sensitive problem, which is growing at the same rapid rate of seismic shifts in varying industries.
- In order to get what they need from higher education, employers must have a good understanding of how the educational system works, starting with making the fire hose (of students prepared for the workforce) and garden hose (job postings and needs) work together.
- Good workforce development rests on a three-legged stool of private-public collaboration where each does what they do best rather than everyone doing everything.

Now let's explore some new methods of collaboration built upon an ecosystem of willing players.

Two

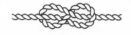

Forming an Ecosystem
of the Willing

CHALLENGE:

How do we deal with a scarcity of
academic resources?

SOLUTION:

We must regionalize higher education resources
to create a portfolio of curricula.

Stability through Agility

Here's a hard problem: How do you get action and innovation out of a confederation of 113 colleges, none of which you directly control because they each have their own local board of trustees in charge of everything, including hiring and firing the institution's leader?

As an appointee of Governor Jerry Brown, I was at the helm of the workforce mission of the California Community Colleges, the largest system of higher education in the nation, with over two million students and then 113 institutions, as its Vice Chancellor of Workforce and Economic Development. While other California public higher education systems, such as the University of California and the California State University, have centralized authority to set direction and hire or fire their chancellors, this was not the case with the California Community Colleges.

Our system office lacked hierarchical power to direct colleges to follow our reform agenda. This was my conundrum, and yet both the legislature and governor's office expected me to drive changes to have these colleges better serve students and employers. To make it even more difficult, I started my role in 2011 during an economic downturn with diminished resources. I suspect many would shy away from stepping into such a situation, but I took the risk and accepted the job because I knew it was my time to serve. As an immigrant who had gained immeasurable opportunity through education, I wanted to hold the door open for the millions of people who looked to the community colleges for social and economic mobility.

Through the rearview mirror, the transformational change I effected seems as if it must have been carefully orchestrated. The truth is that what I learned and achieved was done through experimentation. My team and I succeeded in taking the workforce mission from an afterthought to a state policy priority.

As a result, what started as $100 million under my responsibility became $200 million, then $700 million, and finally exceeded over $1 billion by the time I wrapped up my two-term tenure under Governor Brown. Along the way, we consolidated the two apprenticeship systems into one, integrated the two adult education systems into a single system, and regionalized the community college's approach to career education so that it better served students and employers. We also aligned the monies, metrics, and data to enable the system of community colleges to bring about better career education programs that served students and employers well.

Each time we delivered on what we said we would do, the legislature and governor gave us more funds as a show of confidence and support. For example, when we integrated the two adult education systems, the total funding went from $300 million to $500 million. When we regionalized the approach of community colleges in delivering career education valued by industry, the state infused $200 million of new monies per year of ongoing funds to the cause, equating to $1 billion over five years.

With the funding came the needed influence to move the confederation of colleges along a reform agenda. Despite their initial high level of skepticism and resistance, colleges saw the tangible benefit of working differently—not only getting more resources but also finding increased goodwill once they were better integrated into partnerships within the economic and political infrastructures of their regions.

Codified in what became known as the Strong Workforce Program legislation, my work ultimately fostered an unprecedented level of collaboration and innovation within the system of community colleges. Rebecca Corbin and Ron Thomas highlighted the dynamism that resulted in their book, *Community Colleges as Incubators of Innovation: Unleashing Entrepreneurial Opportunities for Communities and Students.*

Nancy Shulock, longtime critic of the community colleges and then director of the Sacramento State Institute for Higher Education Leadership and Policy, noticed the marked shift in culture and the increased vibrancy. At the annual gathering of all the community college workforce deans across the state, she exclaimed, "It's like I dropped into a different planet!" She saw colleges more energized by a newfound focus on creating opportunity for students and driven by a willingness to collaborate and experiment, thanks to my team's efforts at restructuring the ecosystem.

Big Juan and the Cloud of Self-Doubt

I remember doubting my decision to serve as vice chancellor of the California Community Colleges. In the summer of 2011, after I had been given the political appointment, I traveled to Sacramento from the Bay Area yet again in search of housing for my family to be near my new job. It was hot, hot, hot. On the day of my third visit to the town of Davis, roughly twenty minutes south of Sacramento, it was 96 degrees. I began to question whether it was the right decision to take this risky step of giving up my really good corporate job at PG&E for the lower-paid, time-limited role of vice chancellor. I had heard that the tenure of these political appointments could be fraught with frustration and that many appointees found the work situation difficult given the lack of hierarchical authority over the colleges. Work was done through influence, not control.

I had twenty minutes until my meeting with the real estate agent. Two doors down was a café called the Cloud Forest. It was a small, charming but nondescript place. I decided to step in to get a cold drink. Doubt fogged my mind regarding whether I had made the right career decision. Relocating my family was a big deal.

I stood in line. At the counter, a bubbly young man in his twenties greeted me. After taking my order, he paused, looked up and asked, "Are you a teacher? Did you teach at DeAnza Community College?" I was taken aback. Yes, I had taught at DeAnza many years ago, but that college was located in southern Silicon Valley and a two-and-a-half-hour drive away from where I was standing in the café.

I looked at his face. It was Big Juan, as he called himself, who had taken my small business course. I immediately recalled my time with him and asked, "Big Juan! Did you ever open the candy store that you wanted?" It turns out that Big Juan had moved from Silicon Valley to Virginia, helped his mother open a successful candy store in Annapolis, which he left for her to run, and now he was in the little town of Davis back on the West Coast helping his uncle with the Cloud Forest café.

I was so proud to hear his update. He was the embodiment of opportunity unleashed, and the community college where I had taught small business was a part of what helped propel him on his journey. What was the likelihood that I would have met him at this random moment? That moment affirmed for me that it was my time to serve and the decision to become vice chancellor could help me create opportunity to many others like Big Juan. Interesting enough, I never bumped into Big Juan ever again. He appeared for me at the right time, as I had for him way back, and that chance encounter gave me that needed nudge that affirmed my career decision.

Braiding Efforts

What I achieved during my two terms as vice chancellor and subsequently as executive vice chancellor was essentially the build out of a regionalized and better-networked workforce innovation ecosystem. Previously, each college had thought of itself as the center of its local world. In reality, no single organization had sufficient resources to address all the skills gaps within its regional economy. Hence, employers struggled to find suitable hires, and people found themselves under- or unemployed, even while there were lots of vacant jobs posted. Numerous articles and reports brought to light this conundrum of why it was that those who wanted jobs could not get those good jobs—pointing to the mismatch of skills and jobs.

To begin solving the skills mismatch, it was important for me to recognize that California was a multitude of regional economies, not a single monolithic one, as Tim Rainey, the head of the California Workforce Development Board would say. Los Angeles's economy led in retail and hospitality, while the Inland Empire (comprised of San Bernardino and Riverside counties) and the Central Valley valued manufacturing; biotech mattered to San Diego, and agriculture mattered to the farmers of the South Central region. In cultivating the workforce innovation ecosystem, it mattered less how the regions were carved out. It mattered more that effort was focused on those industries that drove regional economies. Doing so helped focus effort and investment by all those who held resources within that region.

By reorienting the viewpoint to see that a college is one player within a region's wealth of potential partners, we intentionally brought colleges out from siloed positions and networked them to each other and to other partners within the region. In doing so, they found they could braid efforts and resources to do more than each could otherwise achieve on their own.

For example, the San Diego region considered the assessment of labor market research among the community colleges, workforce board, economic development organization, and four-year partners so that, in total, they better understood the unfilled jobs in their county. Previously, each had tried its hand and could only see a partial picture. Effectively, these networks became an innovative and collaborative ecosystem as they discovered themselves solving more complex problems in novel ways together that they could not do alone.

Agility within the Ecosystem

Why do I use the word *ecosystem*? Implied within an ecosystem is the concept of a multitude of players connected to each other, through loosely or tightly affiliated networks. My intent as vice chancellor was to facilitate connectedness among colleges that previously had not existed. I used to say the public systems must dance with one another first before approaching the private sector.

The private sector has no time to sort out partners who can't work together. If collaborating gets too complicated, employers bow out, and you will not have a workforce program if employers are absent from the table. As in all partnerships, key to working together is building trust, and to do so, there needs to be a reason to connect, which I will discuss later.

The diversity inherent in any ecosystem facilitates better adaptation to change. Portions of the ecosystem that are more agile will weather change better and thrive, while the elements that stagnate wither away. John Kotter's 2011 *Harvard Business Review* article astutely states, "While the Hierarchy is as important as it has always been for optimizing work, the Network is where big change happens. It allows a company to spot big opportunities more easily and then change itself to grab them." Except in my situation, it wasn't a company but a large system of 113 public institutions, each one unable to address the skills gap on its own, but collectively, in their regional consortia, they found themselves more resourceful and, surprisingly, more agile.

I remember Steve Linthicum, a longtime faculty member who taught information communications technology (ICT) at one of our community colleges. Highly energetic, creative, if a little gruff, he had already spent a lifetime attracting students into this field of study at his local college. Then, my office put him into a regional role to benefit not only his own institution but fifteen total community colleges in the North/Far North region, which spanned from Sacramento to the Oregon border of California.

Unleashed and networked into the regional ecosystem, he went on to create novel solutions, like the Cyber Patriot program, which exposed high school students to cybersecurity as a field of study. By developing this high school program, he increased enrollment in previously undersubscribed cybersecurity career education programs at colleges. The cybersecurity industry was growing tremendously across the nation but lacked the needed workforce.

Steve's experimentation with the Cyber Patriot program offered students a way to engage in their skillsets and practice them in competition against other schools. The program was so well received that the Governor's Office on Business and Economic Development (GoBiz) provided sponsorship to expand the program. The Bay Area region of twenty-eight community colleges subsequently adopted the proven program in order to boost high school students' interest in collegiate cybersecurity education. Other regions soon replicated the curriculum upon finding that the Cyber Patriot program resonated so strongly with diverse populations of high school students.

The example of the Cyber Patriot program proves that working as a coordinated regional ecosystem, higher education can provide solutions to a broader array of workforce needs. This concept of an ecosystem also applies to companies as well. Beyond that which is proprietary to one company, there is usually commonality in workforce needs across companies and within industries. Combining effort can generate a talent pool with less effort and greater benefit for each party involved.

Stop Blaming—Start Building

Fresno exists in a part of California called the Central Valley, a region rich in agriculture but lacking in job creation. When other regions such as the Bay Area experienced double-digit growth, the Central Valley lagged behind in the single digits; when LA's unemployment was high, Central Valley's rate was higher. People who lived there often traveled hours both ways to find work.

Small and medium-sized businesses that populated the Fresno region liked the low cost of living but struggled to find skilled workers. This was especially true of the small manufacturers who took root in Central Valley. Deborah Nankivell, who led the Fresno Business Council, was a charismatic leader and steward of the region. She and Mike Betts, the CEO of the Betts Company, combined to form an alliance of small manufacturers who sought to join forces to solve the workforce dilemmas they had in common. Coincidentally, my push to regionalize career education at the community colleges was in good timing with their efforts to collaborate.

The Fresno Business Council hosted a gathering of seventy-five small manufacturers with me as the keynote speaker to talk about the importance of manufacturing's middle-skill jobs. *Middle-skill* is the term used to describe roles needing more than a high school degree but less than a bachelor's degree. The gathering showed manufacturers that by working together as an alliance of employers rather than as a single employer, they could better engage the sixteen community colleges in the Central Valley region to produce needed skilled workers.

What started as just seventy-five manufacturers in a room over a decade later became a powerful coalition over 1,000 employers

strong. Eventually called the San Joaquin Valley Manufacturing
Alliance, its 2020 members bragged about having over 105,000
employees and the credit for creating nearly $15 billion of the
Valley's annual GDP.

That region was not alone in galvanizing its employers toward
a concerted effort to collaborate with local educational institutions.
The Manufacturers' Council of the Inland Empire, incubated at
Chaffey, a local community college, had received an offer from
California Steel to donate a building to house student instruction, but
for two years, nothing happened. Once the Inland Empire network
of eleven community colleges started working together rather than
in isolation, they gained the heft to pursue and win a $14 million
federal grant to build a manufacturing center of excellence and
finally take advantage of California Steel's offer.

The fruit of the collaboration was a state-of-the-art training
facility called the InTech Center. For the alliance, the InTech Center
served as a reliable pipeline of much-needed skilled workers, and,
soon enough, employers in the neighboring region of LA started
to tap into the pool.

By organizing themselves into an ecosystem, employers make it
easier for educators to partner with them to reliably deliver people with
the right skills at the right time. Building sector councils and industry
alliances such as those in the Central Valley or in the Inland Empire
regions is a proven, agile approach to workforce development.

Likewise, expanding the collaboration to a regional level
cultivates a more fertile ecosystem for innovation. For employers,
this process creates a marketplace for finding education partners

willing to meet their needs. For educators, creating a new program of study for multiple employers reduces the risk of being dependent on the business cycle of any one company.

I uncovered a secret sauce to forming these ecosystems: start by finding formal and informal leaders whom their community trusts and who can think beyond their parochial interests. In the role of vice chancellor and even previously in my corporate job, when I asked around, there usually was a convergence of opinion on who the thoughtful, trustworthy, and knowledgeable leaders were. This was my playbook at the chancellor's office.

I formed a group, eventually called the Red Team, who would advise me when I began to reshape the community college ecosystem. I started by looking for the workforce deans known for putting the system's interests before their own personal needs. Why red? I could have called it a SWAT Team or Blue Team, but red seemed to signify an urgency for getting the workforce mission right if we were to change lives.

Building the Groundswell

Rock Pfotenhaur was a workforce dean at Cabrillo College. In another life, he would have been a college president. Rock was thoughtful, respected, and knowledgeable. He gathered good people around him, including Kit O'Doherty, who had a gift for facilitating large groups to productively work together. Omid Pourzanjiani, another workforce dean, held this role at Golden West College in Orange County. He came from the technology industry and was the one who would later tell me to "free the data." (More on this in chapter 9.) Rock and Kit were joined by Kari Hammerstrom, Tessa Miley, Jamie Nye, Julie Pekhonen, Mollie Smith, and others.

All of these players came from different regions, yet they all had an understated presence and a good sense of humor in common. All ultimately became trusted connectors whom I marshaled onto the Red Team, hoping they would engage with me in the spirit of stewardship to do what's right for students and the system, and not for direct gains. Also included on the Red Team were the two deans who reported to me, who could benefit from more interactions with practitioners in the field.

I gathered the group to hear what I had heard when I spoke with those who controlled the system's revenues: legislators, the governor's office, the business associations, and others. I had done the prep work of making the rounds to ask stakeholders how they thought our community colleges were doing in regard to our workforce mission. These stakeholders were brutally honest—three pages of fine print honest. The most common gripes that made up their long litany of complaints were familiar: The curricula were irrelevant. Completion rates were low. Colleges weren't responsive enough to the needs of employers.

Bottom line, the community colleges were missing expectations, even if each and every person on the Red Team felt they were doing their very best. The feedback was difficult to digest. We spent our first Red Team meeting with everyone finger-pointing and getting nowhere—fast. Each member was quick to blame the others' failures. I took it all in, which gave me a pounding headache.

We reconvened a few weeks later. Halfway through the meeting,

Rock and Kit made comments that began to turn the conversation. We started to get more productive, homing in on the systemic issues at hand:

- We can't get new curricula through because the state approval process is just too slow.
- We're fine with setting up a few workforce programs, but we don't have the money necessary to set up new equipment and hire new faculty on staff.
- We do have good student outcomes but no one seems to hear about it.
- We want to deliver more student seats but the mandated lower teacher-to-student ratios with the higher faculty cost and large equipment cost, such as in welding or healthcare programs, don't generate enough revenues to get the attention of the college bean counters.

Equal to the overwhelming number of complaints from external stakeholders about our colleges was the number of opinions about how to address them.

I took it all in. Another headache. At our third gathering, I offered up the simple credo of "doing what matters for jobs and the economy" to focus us on the fixes rather than on the criticisms of team members' suggestions. We started reaching out to more workforce deans and faculty to see if our approach resonated. For short, we called our approach "Doing What Matters." Soon, the phrase became a rallying call across all of California's regions.

I knew we'd hit a tipping point when one of my staff members, Robin Harrington, who'd seen twenty-five years' worth of cycles of reforms at the state level and numerous political appointees like me walk the corridors, one day called a college to make an inquiry. As she started to ask how the college went about sunsetting obsolete career education programs, the dean commented, "You must be working on Doing What Matters."

Robin was more than pleased. She said, "Usually the state executive goes into a room and comes out announcing some new marquee that no one has ever heard about." As a long-standing chancellor's office employee, this was her first time to experience a signature program resonating this well with the interest in the field.

Simply by putting an ear to the groundswell of discontent and complaints, and giving words to the underlying pressures at hand, we were finally getting the honest conversations on how to move forward. David Gatewood on the Red Team suggested I get on the road in gatherings we termed *critical conversations* across the state. I co-hosted eleven, which gave me an opportunity to outline the issues, preview the recommendations of the Red Team, and gather more feedback.

In that road map to healing and moving forward, the need to network the colleges into an ecosystem became more clear. They saw themselves as individual contributors rather than as collaborators—and education reform is not an individual but a team sport. I had to forge a path forward that would develop our loose federation of colleges into an ecosystem that was more flexible and agile.

Laying the Bread Crumbs

When I was working in corporate America, wrestling with our company's workforce development needs, I shared the common misperception that there weren't any public resources available to help with my dilemma. However, when I ventured over to the public sector, I found that the real issue was not the amount of available funds, but rather the unproductive, piecemeal way the money flowed.

The Bay Area alone received over $60 million in federal Department of Labor funds in just one year, specifically for use in workforce development. Recipients of these funds operated largely in silos rather than building upon neighboring efforts. Without braiding their efforts, I saw how each recipient had limited reach when it came to creating solutions that helped both employers and communities.

I found the chancellor's office equally guilty of operating within silos. When I started as vice chancellor, I discovered that the two teams in my division issuing grants to encourage small-business development neither spoke nor coordinated with each other. As a result, their grantees saw no need to communicate either.

But what if, I wondered, instead of parceling out the money into hundreds of little grants, we pooled the resources, concentrating funds along three themes? Using the braiding process, we could allocate funds according to industry sectors' priorities by each region, and then deliver technical assistance as needed to build the college capacity to accommodate those priorities.

Rewiring Trust

Restated, we streamlined existing pots of public funding into three categories: strengthening regional ecosystems, investing in industry sectors that mattered to each region, and delivering the technical assistance as needed by colleges to participate. Working alongside me were Debra Jones, Javier Romero, and Nita Patel on my staff. We had a lot of change in management ahead of us.

As a first step, we inventoried the roster of industries that received grant awards from my division in the chancellor's office. We proceeded to refresh the roster and created an updated list of ten industry sectors important to California, including healthcare, advanced manufacturing, information communications technology, biotech and health sciences, water/agriculture/environmental technologies, retail/hospitality/tourism, small business, global trade, and more.

We requested that community colleges and their partners in every region prioritize only five from the list, guided by labor market data and employer input. Rather than spreading resources like peanut butter so that every college got a little but an inadequate amount, we focused our limited resources based on their industry prioritizations. Our intent was to stretch whatever public dollars we had during the economic downturn.

This new approach alone did not beget collaboration. As it turns out, the way the state chancellor's office issued grants influenced a college's choice either to collaborate or compete with other colleges in the region. Before I understood this, I was confounded by why colleges would not better coordinate the volume of students they produced in any program of study, especially since an estimated 60% of students "swirled"—that is, attended at least two community colleges.

Not every college in the region needs to have the same curriculum nor can every college afford to have a full menu of workforce programs. When the need for solar installers was hot, for example, multiple colleges in one region built programs, quickly resulting in an overproduction of students and hence disappointed faculty when students could not find jobs. This cycle kept repeating throughout the system. There needed to be a better mechanism for calibrating how much capacity would be needed to meet the labor market demand. To me, the obvious question to ask colleges was why don't you coordinate more?

The reply that came back from one workforce dean caught me by surprise: "You [the state chancellor's office] pay us to compete." What an interesting observation that, taken at face value, I came to realize was completely spot on. The chancellor's office was running statewide competitions to award grant funds. In doing so, we forced colleges to keep their curricula close to their vests so as not to give others an advantage.

I was trained as an MBA, so, of course, I thought, isn't competition a good thing? Competition has commonly been understood as the way to stimulate higher performance. You've no doubt heard, let the best win. And yet, running the grant competition at a statewide level actually impeded the ability of colleges to work together within a region.

What a head scratcher. How could we get colleges to play together within a region rather than compete with one another? The answer was to change the locus of competition, that is, pit regions against other regions, while at the same time encouraging colleges within each region to collaborate. For example, what if we could get the twenty-eight community colleges of the Los Angeles/ Orange County region to compete with the Bay Area's twenty-eight institutions?

Twenty-something colleges is an extraordinary amount of higher education capacity to parlay toward solving workforce issues. Could rewiring how colleges thought about each other (i.e., become collaborators instead of competitors) result in better career education programs for students and employers? At that time, colleges in Los Angeles barely met with one another, but instead stood at a distance, fighting fiercely for resources. In the Bay Area, only ten of the twenty-eight met together and did so just once a year.

Changing the flow of money would not be easy, but doing so could inexorably open the path to new levels of collaboration on which we would lay the bread crumbs of trust. No doubt, the greatest challenge we faced in building a regional ecosystem was getting the colleges to play together. This was an age-old problem rooted in prior policy incentives that rewarded colleges to compete, not only for grant dollars but also for student enrollment.

My staff and I, along with the Red Team, set the change into motion. We had no new funds, so we looked at redeploying existing resources. We stopped issuing statewide competitions in which there could be only one winner. Instead, we divvied up the monies into seven regional pots and guaranteed a winner for each geographic footprint. The first grant was one that could only be won by a community college that served as lead applicant if 60% of their colleagues in the region signed on to the common practice outlined for grantees. No college was forced to participate. But, in joining forces and pursuing the same grant, those colleges that applied together would have no choice but to work collaboratively, serving the needs of the region and not just their own institutions.

Of course, many college leaders were unhappy with these new terms primarily because they were good at winning in the past, and any change to the grant process injected uncertainty for them. Yet, in spite of the significant pushback, one winning application was awarded per region. The colleges that joined along in their region's winning proposal all benefited financially.

We issued a second grant where there would be a guaranteed winner in each region again, but this time 100% of the community colleges in the region had to sign on. Miraculously, one grant was awarded in every region. We did this again for the third grant, reinforcing what we desired. The details of what these grants entail were less important. Our goal was to create a reason for community colleges to network themselves to each other, for partnership can only begin with trust. The competition gave these institutions an incentive to meet one another and collaborate.

With the grants acting as bread crumbs, faculty members and administrators who followed the trail would eventually find themselves in a newly networked regional ecosystem, better able to generate resources and coordinate education capacity. The bread crumbs gave them all a reason to talk and work with one another.

In 2018, Amazon Web Services (AWS) recognized the power behind this expanded type of ecosystem that was already organized and ready for collaboration when they announced a partnership with the nineteen Los Angeles community colleges. AWS would release its cloud-technician curriculum to these community colleges to offer degrees to their students. All the same community colleges additionally committed to setting up relationships with their high school feeders to stairstep students into these industry-valued training programs. AWS's corporate customers who struggled to find talent would soon have a reliable workforce pipeline flowing. Of the many possibilities across the country, the network of nineteen community colleges already working together appealed to AWS.

For the first time ever, the colleges in Los Angeles, that until then had been notorious for their competitive edge, were actually playing together in the same sandbox. With such a feat already under our belts, there was no telling what opportunities to collaborate the future held.

In the next chapter, I will take a look at how and why more corporations such as AWS can utilize their curricula to fill the gaps of specialized skills.

CHAPTER HIGHLIGHTS

- An ecosystem of the willing offers solutions otherwise not available when one organization works alone.
- To form an ecosystem, find trusted formal and informal leaders of organizations who act beyond their individual interests.
- We should consider regions an effective unit for pooling effort and resources in response to workforce needs.
- Braiding resources and effort yields a far greater impact than spreading them like peanut butter across a region.
- By shaping the rules for how public money gets distributed, we can institute transformational change.
- The way funds flow shapes whether institutions collaborate or compete with one another.
- By intentionally connecting community colleges into networks, we can build trust among unlikely partners.
- Networked community colleges function like an ecosystem whose strength lies in its agility and adaptability.

Three

Surfing the Wave
of the Future

CHALLENGE:

How do we crank out the workforce
pipeline to benefit employers?

SOLUTION:

Employers must have an active role
in reshaping the curriculum.

Following the Bellwethers of Innovation

Many moons ago, I held a strategy job at Digital Island, a high-tech start-up with headquarters in Honolulu, the city where I grew up. I was thrilled that Hawaii's economy was expanding beyond tourism and also excited by the idea that my new job returned me regularly to my childhood home every time I visited the main office in person. My friends and family eagerly volunteered to come along with me on business trips. Of course, I hadn't taken into account being miserable stuck inside an office most of the day, wistfully looking out the window while my travel companions got to soak up the sun.

Just as my expectations about this aspect of the job had been incorrect, so were some of the assumptions I had held about the workplace in general. As I quickly came to realize, being at Digital Island showed me technology's uncanny ability to disrupt my understanding of the world, putting my assumptions to the test. In this regard, I experienced a sharp learning curve.

I was in my early thirties then, just a few years out of a double masters-degree program at Stanford. High tech was hot, hot, hot all around me. Digital Island was a company at the forefront of internet infrastructure deployment, and it attracted young, whip-smart techies at the leading edge of the field. Doug was a twenty-something systems engineer in our office who barely had facial hair, but he had grown up with the browser; whereas, I had not. One day, our team was facing a question about encryption export. I proceeded to flip through my rolodex of contacts—yes, you read that correctly—to reach someone who might be able to answer the question. I was quite proud of my extensive professional network contained on those neat little 2x3 cards. Of course,

I didn't realize how behind the times I was until Doug looked up quizzically and asked, "Why would you do that? Just go to the internet for the answer." It had only been a few years since graduate school, when I remember the first browsers appeared on campus. Yet in the eyes of this young techie, my world view was already sadly outdated. The dawning of the Age of Information was turning me, a thirty-something rising executive who had grown up without the internet, into a dinosaur.

If you read the introduction of this book, you know I lived through a merger and acquisition (M&A) where seniority was rendered meaningless. Here, I was experiencing firsthand how career longevity and years of education meant nothing to the Dougs of this world. Technology was a tough teacher.

Playing with Disruption

Similar to what I experienced with M&A after graduate school, not to mention the war I had experienced in my childhood, technology has a way of upturning the normal landscape. Perhaps you too have found the changes disorienting. When it came to the workplace, I found that certain norms had been rendered outdated, including my treasured rolodex of experts, once a valuable asset for career success.

In the face of disruptive forces, I was given a choice: I could try to push back the change or I could look at the revised landscape as an opportunity. You can guess which choice I made. I watched with interest how young Doug did things and considered him a bellwether for the new skillsets that would over time become indispensable.

In contrast to Doug, who embraced the internet, the CEO of Bell South, the company that acquired my California-based telecommunications company Pacific Bell, had dismissed the internet as yet another passing fad of the West Coast. It turns out that Doug, in spite of his youth, was much wiser.

Back then, it was internet adoption. Now it's the advent of self-driving cars, telemedicine, cryptocurrency, block chain, competency-based online learning, and virtual/augmented reality. The list goes on, but the disruptive nature of these new frontiers is the same.

I recently interviewed innovation leader Dr. Soon Joo Gog for my WorkforceRx podcast. She leads Singapore's SkillsFuture agency and shapes how her country invests in and responds to changing demands on skills. One key strategy for her is seeking innovation leaders—the organizational version of Doug—to see how their use of technology affects the workflow and, hence, workforce skills. One of my favorites of her stories has to do with Changi Airport Terminal 4, which is fully automated with robots instead of live human beings to check you in and handle luggage. (The terminal is even equipped with Jetson-style dustbins [trash cans]!):

As Dr. Gog said on my podcast:

> [B]ecause of the operational model changes, it will impact the kind of workforce within. There will be a reduction of counter service staff, but they will require more experienced and empathetic customer service officers who roam around the whole airport to help those who look lost or who seem to be needing some help.

They will not be serving just one single customer. So, the kind of training required for the customer service officer is very different. Those who receive the data on the back end will be very different. Those who will be observing the dashboard, looking at the whole picture, from the cleanliness to other matters at a smart airport, will be very different. The maintenance team will be very different. If you come to Changi airport today, you will see robots cleaning the whole airport moving around on their own. The dustbin itself is a smart dustbin because it will signal someone when it is almost full and requires emptying.

Disruptions show little deference to job seniority. Weathering changes requires looking around the corner toward harbingers like young Doug and Changi Airport Terminal 4 to glean insights into the future of work. Later in my career, I would leverage these signals to decode for others, in a more inclusive model of workforce development and recovery, what skillsets could lead them to opportunity.

Moving at the Speed of Need

After earning my workforce development stripes in the private sector, I stepped into the public sector as vice chancellor of the California Community Colleges, driving the system's workforce mission. With 113 institutions when I started, there was great unevenness across their landscape of good workforce education. And, unlike general education programs whose classical curricula in

English and math changed slowly, career programs needed constant updating to keep up with the times. I urged my community college brethren to rethink and speed up their processes with this mantra: We must move at the speed of business.

Traditionally, taking a year to analyze the labor market and another two to finalize the curriculum meant that students would not begin to enroll in training for a particular position until year three, and graduates would not be ready to hit the job market until years four or five. By then, the job opportunity most likely would have come and gone. Faculty and administrators who had missed the entire business cycle complained, "We did what employers asked but, in the end, they didn't hire."

Later in this chapter, I'll reemphasize the need for agile curriculum-approval processes to keep up with industry trends. For now, it's important to recognize the vital role that timing plays in the collaboration between education and industry to create agile processes responsive to employer needs. This was one of the most vital lessons I tried to remind my colleagues of again and again. When they got it and set themselves up for a speedier curriculum-approval process, colleges with previously languishing career programs started finding themselves relevant to industry— and to students. With the support of industry, not only did students benefit but, from the goodwill generated, employers in communities also became overtly supportive when ballot measures sought out tax dollars to fund facility construction at local community colleges.

Accessing Opportunity through Education

In January 2020, I launched a new nonprofit in healthcare workforce development named Futuro Health—just three months ahead of the global pandemic. Little did I know that, in my role as CEO, moving at the pace of business would no longer suffice. The COVID-19 pandemic disruption suddenly required my team to move at a new pace: the speed of need.

Futuro Health was founded with a $130 million commitment from Kaiser Permanente, a large multi-state managed-care health system, and SEIU–United Healthcare Workers West, a major labor union with almost 100,000 hospital workers as its members. Futuro Health's mission is to increase the health and wealth of communities by growing the largest network of allied health workers in the nation.

If you're wondering what occupations comprise allied health, imagine the range of care providers whom you would come in contact with upon being in a car accident—from the emergency medical technician who drives up in an ambulance, the medical assistant who handles your paperwork at the hospital, the radiology technician who takes your X-ray and so on. Minus the doctors and administrators, the rest of your interactions are likely with allied health workers, encompassing an estimated 65% of healthcare occupations.

After serving two terms as a political appointee with the California Community Colleges under Governor Brown and growing public investment in workforce education under my responsibility from $100 million to over $1 billion, I accepted the role of CEO. In Futuro Health, I saw a whiteboard on which I could explore novel solutions to persistent and pervasive problems that plagued healthcare workers who wanted a better life and needed to access opportunity through education.

Before Futuro Health got its name, I worked with SEIU–UHW and commissioned four focus groups across the state, including one Spanish-speaking forum since this language is spoken by 39% of households in California. During these gatherings, I heard common themes. Adults wanted a chance at a better career and a better life for their families but did not know how to get there from their current situation. Even for those who had broken into healthcare, they were stuck on the first entry-level career position, burdened by the enormity of their student debt that also kept them from getting the advanced training needed for higher-paying jobs. Listening to these voices, I began to formulate a unique strategy for Futuro Health.

One direction I considered was whether Futuro Health should itself be an educational institution. Our funding gave us an option to seek accreditation if we wanted to do so. After all, Kaiser Permanente already had formed the Kaiser Permanente School of Allied Health Sciences and the Kaiser Permanente Bernard J. Tyson School of Medicine. However, this strategy required a lag period of years to gain accreditation, in which time the yield of students would be limited, topping out at hundreds and not the thousands needed to fill the workforce gap.

According to the US Bureau of Labor Statistics, employment in healthcare occupations is projected to grow 15% from 2019 to 2029, adding an estimated 2.4 million new jobs in order to adequately take care of the nation's aging population. Allied health jobs, which approximate 65% of healthcare jobs, are projected to grow at twice the rate of other occupations during that time. In California alone, an estimated 500,000 allied health workers would be needed on the front line of care for the growing and graying population.

By 2030, California's population is projected to reach 44.1 million, and the total number of adults age sixty-five and older is projected to grow from 5 million in 2014 to 8.6 million in 2030. This projection is particularly foreboding, considering the fact that Americans over sixty-five use more health services than any other age group.

A persistent shortage of skilled workers will mean that hundreds of thousands of positions will remain unfilled. Given the immensity of the allied health worker shortage, we needed a strategy that would beget scale. Futuro Health would launch initially in California despite its national scope, using the Golden State as a good test of whether we could design agile workforce development solutions at scale to tackle the countrywide structural skills shortage.

An Agile Approach to Workforce Development

Aiming for scale, I decided to adapt practices from a playbook I had developed during my days with the California Community Colleges. That system was the largest higher education system in the nation, now with 116 institutions serving over 2 million students. Across all the reforms implemented while there, I found fertile ground and scalable solutions in building out an innovative ecosystem of partners. Once cultivated, this ecosystem shared common interests, braided its resources, and shepherded in an unprecedented level of collaboration, experimentation, and adaptation.

One community college faculty member, amazed at the new

agility of these college administrations, said I was teaching dinosaurs to dance. I knew how easy it was to be rendered a dinosaur by the disruptive forces of young Dougs and Changi Airport Terminal 4s. By cultivating an ecosystem, we could move seemingly large and otherwise plodding public systems to tackle systemic workforce deficits with greater buoyancy and ease.

With that playbook in hand, I launched Futuro Health with the mission to increase the health and wealth of communities by growing the largest network of allied health workers in the nation. In his May 2021 publication, veteran higher education journalist Paul Fain observed, "The new Futuro Health is an unusual model worth watching, according to a wide range of observers. It's also a complex solution to an enormous societal challenge."

Futuro Health would become the curator and cultivator of the training ecosystem, inviting higher education, student support, employers, and technology partners to play together to create educational opportunities for adults on their journey toward an industry-valued healthcare credential.

These students, who averaged thirty years in age, had very compli-cated lives, juggling family, work, limited finances and social supports, and other demanding obligations. In 2020, some would experience homelessness from the rampant fires that raged across California, while others would face sickness firsthand and the deaths of loved ones from COVID-19. Those circumstances piled on top of the normal issues that can derail students, ranging from childcare to transportation.

Futuro Health's ecosystem of partners came together to contribute to a more agile approach to workforce development. Right out of the gate, the board of Futuro Health approved our collaboration with six accredited higher education institutions with good track records for specific healthcare programs of study. All these colleges offered adult-friendly programs, which meant they were usually fully or mostly online, and any in-person portions of the curriculum would be sensitive to work schedules.

To provide live student supports, which is particularly important for the diverse student base we served, we invited Inside Track, a national nonprofit led by Kai Drekmeier specializing in student coaching, to provide the high-touch elements necessary for our enrollees to persist on their education journey. By our one-year anniversary, we enrolled 1,691students tuition-free, a number that significantly surpassed our 1,500 goal, and the student body equivalent of a small college.

Kai was pleasantly surprised by this success since 2020 was a year when most nonprofit organizations missed their goals or were barely hanging on due to the pandemic. At the same time, my board was thrilled to have created the opportunity for an inclusive student population that averaged thirty years in age, who were 76% female, 87% ethnically diverse, and 36% bilingual. The percentage of women is of note because the pandemic created what some referred to as the "she-cession," with females dropping out of the workforce from bookended complications caused by telework and children staying at home for school.

Futuro Health launched to strong media coverage in January 2020. Three months later, the world went into quarantine with the first wave of COVID-19 infections. My board chair and vice chair, whose day jobs were in healthcare and hospitals, voiced trepidation and concern. Frontline healthcare workers, still lacking specific upskilling training, were not ready for the surge in COVID-19 cases.

The questions were these: What were the fundamentals of the disease's progression? How should healthcare workers don and doff protective personal equipment (PPE) and work with respirators? Given the conversion of all beds for use by the ICU, how would workers in sub-acute environments pivot to patient care within acute environments that housed sicker individuals?

Many frontline workers had not touched these skills since they were initially trained and licensed. The healthcare community was facing dire circumstances, and my board hoped that Futuro Health could help.

This was Futuro Health's first major test of agility. We had only two and a half weeks to develop the training curriculum before a significant surge in infection was expected to hit our state. That's when I realized that the speed of need is even faster than the pace of business. Could we transition from our original plans and deliver in time? Would the disruption render our young organization a dinosaur already?

Fortunately, in our quest for relevance, we already had cultivated an ecosystem of partners who were all willing to roll up their sleeves and do their parts. Pima Medical Institute, an accredited higher education provider headquartered in Arizona with satellite campuses in California, was among our key players. Their CEO, Fred Freedman, raised his hand and volunteered to develop the needed training program. Fred would donate his organization's curriculum if Futuro Health could host the content on our own learning management system. Futuro Health agreed and implemented the learning management system Canvas to house the instructional content in record time. The Canvas software company lowered their licensing price to cost as an act of public service.

Kaiser Permanente, our founder, pledged experts on their staff to review and do quality assurance on the new curriculum. SEIU–UHW and The Education Fund organized an email campaign to reach frontline healthcare workers to generate awareness for the free training. This was trial-by-fire for our partners and my newly formed management team.

My technology team, led by Anthony Dalton, also put their prowess to the test. Not only did they implement Canvas as our learning management system, but they showed the software vendor a few tricks for how we streamlined the student experience. Debbie Yaddow, a former nurse and allied health dean who came out of retirement to work for Futuro Health, treated the situation like a patient in triage, calling on multiple stakeholders to review draft training content in rapid successive deadlines.

Just in the nick of time, we launched the training within the two-and-a-half-week window. Healthcare workers began learning and logging digital completion badges as they raced through the training. Over 4,000 frontline healthcare workers across twenty states took the coursework in time. In the end, Futuro Health stayed relevant by moving at the speed of need.

A few months later, I asked my board to reflect on what they thought would be permanent effects of the pandemic on the healthcare workforce and what systems and practices would revert.

Hands down, the industry experts declared that telehealth is here to stay. Use rate of telehealth for primary-care appointments had hovered in the teens prior to the pandemic. Once the shelter-in-place mandate was enforced, telehealth became the only choice, and adoption skyrocketed to above 80%. I knew we had to adjust Futuro Health's road map of training programs if we wanted to stay relevant within this nationwide disruption.

Looking around the country, we found a fifteen-week, fully online, quality program at the University of Delaware called Advanced Telehealth Coordinator, whose curriculum equipped healthcare clinic staff with the skillsets needed to set up telehealth as a service. The program existed before the pandemic and had been well received by the professionals who previously attended, but it had limited seats. Our partnership with the University of Delaware identified ways to create more seats, and Futuro Health was able to connect struggling community health centers with training just in time. The first cohort of 162 healthcare staff members who attended the program experienced an 87% completion rate because the training was so timely.

Beyond the Comfort Zone

If you haven't already noticed, I'm someone who loves solving problems that lack a good playbook. By the time I was asked to build Futuro Health and serve at its helm, I had already designed novel work-force development solutions at PG&E and the California Community Colleges that gained national recognition. In both these situations, the workforce issues were evident and long standing to stakeholders.

Were the solutions that I pursued those that no one had ever thought of before? Not at all. Colleagues would tell me later that they recognized elements as ideas they had previously considered and thrown around, but could not get off the ground. It wasn't that my moves had never been thought of before. The secret to my strategies was how I combined design with the practical maneuvers to make them happen. My knack for developing agile new playbooks had to do with how I combined components into a comprehensive solution that was attractive not just to one partner, but to many.

How did I learn to do this? Trial and error helped, as did my knack for finding out-of-the-box solutions to seemingly unresolvable dilemmas as a child refugee. Having been displaced by war, my parents did not know the difference between possibilities deemed standard and those that would be too much of a reach. After all, they fled their home country and restarted our family in a new one. They harbored fewer expectations than someone who understood the norms; hence, I grew up less sensitive to the possibility of failure and more open to taking risks. In this way, having the whiteboard of passed-down expectations wiped clean from war is liberating, I suppose.

The penchant for tackling the seemingly improbable was already in me in the early 2010s when I was working in workforce development at PG&E. The company's welding supervisor—I believe his name was Samuel—found himself desperately needing to replenish the division's talent pool of arc welders, a highly specialized cohort of technicians in the utility industry. Highly skilled compared to their hobbyist counterparts, these craftspeople could weld together large gas pipelines while hanging upside down in torrential rain.

Indeed, they were a special breed.

A grandfatherly type in his early sixties, and aged from the hard work of welding, Samuel talked about how he'd tried to connect with the community colleges through the Rotary Club, but the leads had always come to a dead end. He explained that for a really long time, the company had not needed to hire new welders and therefore did not keep up relations with colleges. Just as I couldn't have predicted that my rolodex would become obsolete, Samuel hadn't predicted that these programs would wither from social and industrial changes that ultimately had led to a shortage of talent. Now the company's number of welders was down to a meager twenty-five, a risky handful compared to the onetime high of around 120.

By the time I spoke with him, Samuel had grown frustrated with repeatedly trying without success to collaborate with the education sector. As the Director of Workforce Development, I'd seen this problem before. The problem was not that the empty talent pool was too large to fill; it was that the ecosystem was not structured to make it easy to find the right workers and resources. Samuel needed to expand beyond local colleges in his backyard to include other collaborators. I made a mental note of this as something needing fixing at large scale.

With the help of Catherine Swenson who specialized in continuing education with the community colleges, I scanned the range of higher education partners in the state that had welding programs. Butte College, a community college upstate, had a welding program that was good, though not exactly what Samuel needed. While the faculty were strong, student interest flagged. Welding really wasn't a career on anyone's mind.

We agreed to train Butte's welding faculty in the skills they needed to teach their students by inviting them to the PG&E Training Center. As you may remember from chapter 1, this was the same tactic I employed with Dave Meisel to ready the seven community colleges with brand-new electric vehicle maintenance skills needed by his mechanics.

In order to reverse the declining student interest in welding, PG&E joined with the college faculty to generate excitement and enrollment. This meant rolling out PG&E's big bright blue state-of-the-art technology vehicles to park at Butte College career fairs and sending company welders to participate in demonstrations and talks.

In a short time, word got around about the company's endorsement and sponsorship, and enrollment grew in the welding program. Student quality became more competitive, to the delight of the instructors as well as Samuel. Once again, private-public collaboration proved an undeniable win-win.

As we saw in the case of the electric vehicle fleet in chapter 1, the solution to a talent puddle lies is finding an ecosystem of willing partners. In both cases of Dave Meisel's mechanics and Samuel's welders, the private-public partnership unlocked capabilities and resources to address their workforce problem in more agile ways than either could do on their own. Without a doubt, employer endorsement of education programs goes a long way to generate interested, qualified applicants.

The Role of Assets in a Gig Economy

For every juncture at which a disruption occurs, we must think about looking around the corner at how skills will change in the near future. Likewise, if we want an inclusive talent pool, good workforce development must decode for others how to access upcoming opportunity.

Let's look at the gig economy. According to the Gig Economy Data Hub, "More than a quarter of workers participate in the gig economy in some capacity. Some measures of the gig economy include any worker who engages in nontraditional work in any capacity—online or offline, with regular or occasional participation, and for primary or supplemental earnings. This includes workers who hold traditional full-time jobs in addition to gigs, as well as those who only do gig work."

Make no mistake: the rise of the gig economy is drastically changing the face of work as we know it, and the education-related disparities that I have already discussed only contribute to the escalating pace of that change. The recent British ruling to classify Uber drivers—over 70,000 of them—as workers entitled to certain, albeit restricted, benefits is a huge indicator of how workforce norms can shift dramatically in the global gig economy.

The question of what constitutes an "employee" has led to legal tensions in many other jurisdictions, including California. New forms of work will challenge existing human infrastructures, including not only who gets benefits but also who qualifies for unemployment benefits. Most important for us is one big implication: if gig platforms are where people are finding work, then how do we decode for others how to participate in it?

For many workers, engaging in the gig economy represents the way to set your own schedule. For others, it's a way not to spend time and effort working for a boss you don't respect, but instead to be your own boss. In some cases, this benefit of autonomy can lead workers into situations in which they feel they are being exploited (like irregular workers who cannot influence their gig schedule and are subject to the last-minute cancellation of the work hours that they need to pay their bills).

Freelance work can also lead people into work arrangements entirely outside the traditional boss-worker system. In the 2020 US presidential election, candidate Andrew Yang based his campaign around the suggestion that citizens should all receive a UBI, or Universal Basic Income (also referred to as "guaranteed income"). He wasn't successful in getting elected to the presidency but did receive a great deal of attention and support.

The UBI idea is appealing to many with nascent pilots already under way in cities like Stockton and Los Angeles. Marina Gorbis, executive director of the Institute for the Future, has suggested that the idea be tweaked by looking at the problem more deeply. Gorbis points out that what leads to inequality is not necessarily a skewed distribution of income but of assets. Therefore, in her view, we should be looking at universal basic assets, rather than at income.

She writes:

Assets aren't just cars and money: They're the primary resources that people can leverage to generate income. Ownership or access to assets—such as equity shares, certain types of land, education, and social connections—is what gives people the foundation to generate an income and therefore create more wealth. For example, if they inherit financial capital, they can invest the money in the stock market, buy a home, and pay for a good education, thus leveraging their inherited assets to generate more wealth and a higher income. If they have access to health insurance, they are able to take care of their physical and mental selves, which makes it easier for them to work and earn money. If they own a house or an apartment, they can put it on Airbnb and earn extra income, or sell it. The more assets people have, the more they can leverage them to generate even more assets, and the more income they can eventually bring in.

The implications for the shifting world of work are impossible to ignore. In Gorbis's gig-economy example, a house or apartment is an asset that can lead to income via Airbnb. That's absolutely true, but we shouldn't forget that by no means are all assets as physically tangible as a house. Knowledge and skills—including the skills to manage your professional reputation on gig platforms—are assets too. And they are assets at a huge premium in this age of the gig economy's ascendancy.

Online platforms such as Uber, TaskRabbit, Upwork, and Fiverr increasingly connect people with work opportunities for pay. I, myself, was someone who always experienced full-time employment and therefore never sought any freelance jobs for income.

To get a closer glimpse into the next economy, I hosted a field trip to Silicon Valley a few years back for my California Community Colleges advisory body, the Economic and Workforce Development Advisory Committee. Dylan Hendricks, who worked at the Institute for the Future, agreed to guide our group, which included ten industry representatives, ten community college CEOs, faculty representatives, and labor union, philanthropy, and social justice advocates, on visits with pioneers of gig-economy innovation.

Upwork was among the handful of organizations we toured, with a shockingly large and impressive cache of 12 million gig workers ready for hire around the world. That was back then. Five years later, Upwork now boasts 18 million registered freelancers and 5 million registered clients, making it the largest freelancer marketplace in the world. The twenty-something manager at Upwork explained how her clients sourced freelancers using the platform and how big companies such as Accenture and IBM were establishing enterprise-level contracts with them.

The latter caught my attention. Once again, my spider sense went off. If large, established companies were sourcing from Upwork, gig platforms soon would become mainstream. What was happening on the Upwork platform was a harbinger of things to come. I added Upwork to my mental list of disruptors that already included young Doug and Changi Airport Terminal 4.

Traditional ways of seeking work, such as preparing detailed resumes and earning degrees, do not have the same cachet in the gig marketplace. Rather, a gig worker's golden ticket to winning a client is a standout online profile, which includes excellent client ratings, a tally of repeat users, a portfolio of sample work, a punchy byline, a star-quality photo, and skill badges. Learning this, I wondered how many college graduates knew that their likely first job would depend on these elements. The daunting question that followed was this: How does someone get their first gig in an ocean of 18 million competitors? The rising gig economy was yet another wave of futurity that everyone would have to ride.

In the same the way that I had watched young Doug at Digital Island act as a bellwether for the Information Age, I studied with curiosity our Upwork tour guide as she described her own company. She explained that Upwork believed so much in the gig economy that the company made it a point to practice what it preached. Out of all the workers it employed, 700 were contractors retained through its platform, and only 300 employees were actually on payroll. In other words, there were twice as many gig opportunities as there were traditional full-time positions at the company.

Is this a signal of the future of work? Will future generations of college graduates work for a company through a platform as the primary way to get hired? If the current trend continues, this will likely be the case.

The Institute for the Future shared with us an experiment one of their teams had conducted. Marina Gorbis, the Institute's CEO who hosted portions of the tour, explained that her organization produced research reports as a core product. Her team wondered whether research reports could be done entirely through talent sourced via a gig platform. They pursued a demonstration project to find out. Marina explained how her team broke down the layers of research and writing and, for each phase, sourced impressive researchers and editors to perform each step. The conclusion affirmed that indeed a quality report could be created through use of gig talents. The aha idea from the changed workflow would be to alter who the Institute kept on payroll; instead of having researchers and writers on its permanent staff, the team concluded that it would be more advantageous to have the internal hires act as project managers to source and orchestrate gig talent.

Alleviating Unconscious Bias for Future Gig Workers

On a platform, reputation management would be a key skill important for entry-level gig workers to learn. If clients rated you poorly, prospective ones would be reticent to give you a chance. I wondered how students, including those coming from diverse communities with fewer resources for career advice and less social capital to teach them the tricks of the trade, would learn these norms. Who was decoding for them the first step toward creating a reputation and portfolio when they started out? Not likely their parents, who grew up without gig platforms. At worst, these young men and women would have no knowledge of these platforms and miss out while others accumulated new-economy work experience.

Needless to say, the Upwork tour was eye-opening for me, as well as for the industry and college leaders who joined the tour. The visit to

Silicon Valley gave us a peek around the corner into the future of work. As usual, I was immediately compelled to do something to equalize the playing field. Whether I personally would become a gig worker was irrelevant. This was an economy with rewards for those who understood its norms.

Once back at the chancellor's office, I had my office issue a grant solicitation to find twenty community colleges willing to work together to create a new certificate that would introduce students to entrepreneurship and work in the gig economy. Chuck Eason, workforce dean at Solano Community College who had an expertise in entrepreneurship, led the execution. He believed in students' ability to opt for the flexibility and freedom of choosing their own hours by starting their own businesses.

The certificate Self-Employment Pathway into the Gig Economy launched and included introductory coursework on entrepreneurship, an overview, and experimentation with the use of tech platforms, as well as mentoring to help students launch or expand their own businesses. The coursework reminds students that, in order to be successful, gig workers needed to make sure they earn enough money to cover living costs as well as the often overlooked expenses of healthcare and retirement. This certificate decoded for all students the new norms, equalizing the playing field for everyone who wished to participate.

Building Timely Curricula

AI, advanced robotics, health informatics, precision medicine, internet of things (IoT) and so on—all of these technological frontiers are constantly changing the skillsets needed to stay relevant in different industries. When higher education can incorporate these changes into its curricula, colleges provide the value of decoding these developments for a wider swath of students. Timeliness is key. While it's true that certain subjects such as math and history don't change much on a year-to-year basis, workforce programs by definition are utterly time-sensitive—at the mercy of ever-moving and accelerating technological trends.

Colleges tend to be timid about introducing new career education programs because of the risk involved. Liberal arts courses like English often require not much more than a wallboard and books as instructional supplies. Workforce programs, in contrast, usually require students to practice workplace skills. This type of training demands a capital investment that enables colleges to acquire physical equipment and supplies to allow students to practice, for example, fixing vehicles on actual engines, building computers out of piece parts, or providing care on high-tech mannequin patients that emote pain.

Keeping career education programs relevant means a constant cycle of financing to sustain career relevance. Employers who pro-actively partner early with education on curriculum development often can reduce a college's reluctance to invest, by reducing the perceived risk. Even better, when employers can contribute some of the equipment necessary to start a program or even loan an expert to serve as adjunct faculty, colleges can more easily offer the coursework. Even industrial gear a few generations old can have relevance for training purposes.

Looking around the corner, what about next-generation skills? I interviewed Shalin Jyotishi on my WorkforceRx podcast. Shalin is a world economic forum global shaper and senior analyst with New America Foundation, a policy think-and-do tank. Shalin spoke of how federal government invested research and development (R&D) dollars into photonics, autonomous vehicles, and other manufacturing futures and strategically embedded workforce development into the charters of those efforts.

I was fortunate to have firsthand experience with one of these federal investments through NextFlex, a private-public partnership focused on flexible hybrid electronics technology operating in the heart of Silicon Valley. Together with workforce development dean Lena Tran at the San Jose–Evergreen Community College District, NextFlex came up with a *Shark Tank*-like contest to expose highly diverse high school and community college students to future manufacturing opportunities generated by embedding technologies into fabrics.

In the NextFlex competition, student teams would come up with product concepts that used the new technology, prepare and pitch the business concepts on stage, and receive feedback from industry experts. Sitting there in the seventh row of the school auditorium among the industry judges, I was deeply impressed by the acumen and creativity of these young women and men. They inspired me. One team, for instance, came up with the idea of embedding the NextFlex technology into baby booties and onesies to detect and possibly prevent sudden infant death syndrome (SIDS). Compression socks with adjustable firmness levels to accelerate healing were another unique brainchild of their creative energies.

From that seat in the auditorium, I pictured many of these students going on through the science, technology, engineering, and math (STEM) pipeline as researchers and technicians. NextFlex is only one of many innovative collaborations between industry and education, funded by the federal government, that I've been able to witness that bridge the skills gap for highly specialized fields. In the next chapter, we'll explore how we as policy makers, industry leaders, and educators can scale good practices like these to prepare for the future workforce.

CHAPTER HIGHLIGHTS

- Technology is disrupting the familiar landscape of work, now faster and more drastically than ever.
- We need to look around the corner and invest in changing worker skills in order to keep up with the times.
- Innovation leaders can be bellwethers of how technology will change workflows and skillsets.
- Timeliness is essential to stay relevant in a private-public partnership. Keeping curriculum updated is key and involves the engagement of employers early and often.
- Moving at the speed of need requires matching market demands with workforce demands, starting with the timeliness of curriculum.
- Creating a talent pool from a talent puddle lies in finding an ecosystem of willing partners.
- Partnerships unlock capabilities and resources to address their workforce problem in more agile ways than any one entity could do on its own.
- Employer endorsement and sponsorship of higher education programs go a long way to generate interest and enrollment.
- Good workforce development must decode for communities how to access opportunity.
- Skills needed to function in the norms of the gig economy will be indispensable in the future of work.

Four

Removing Barriers for Inclusive Growth

CHALLENGE:

How can we make career opportunities
more reachable and skills development
more ongoing to the employed?

SOLUTION:

Employers must make on-the-job
learning more affordable and flexible
and skillsets more portable.

Taking the Talent to the Next Level

In prior chapters, I pointed out the need for organizations to widen the talent funnel. Now let's explore ways to develop that talent once it enters an organization.

As a board member of the National Skills Coalition (NSC), an organization committed to inclusive, high-quality skills training, I help advocate for federal and state policy changes aimed at bolstering local economies. More importantly, we work to level the playing field for members of countless underrepresented communities and keep them growing in their skills training.

The NSC's advice on smart legislation and practices is largely informed by firsthand practitioners who are on the ground, working to bridge the gap between diverse populations who want jobs and companies facing a shortage of skilled employees. Employers can make educational resources available to workers, but what happens if employees don't use them? Considering the industry need for skilled employees and the high cost of training investment, the choice to opt out of company- and government-subsidized education benefits was a conundrum that the NSC was determined to solve.

A few years ago, I was in a conference session hosted by the NSC that discussed the different ways in which companies could support upskilling employees. One Midwestern CEO, Nathan, shared how his manufacturing company's tuition reimbursement program had until recently engaged only a small number of its employees. Tuition benefits offer employees a way to access higher education on the company's dime, but usually on the employee's own time. With the low volume of takers, did this mean his employees were uninterested in improving their own skills and upward mobility? Or was it the required time investment that made the option unappealing?

After talking to his workers about the education support program and a series of probing questions, Nathan discovered that the company's low enrollment stemmed not from lack of interest but from two main issues that I've since seen over and over in adult skills training.

The first hindrance to enrollment was a lack of flexibility in the delivery of the training; adult workers have complicated schedules and life commitments that make it challenging to find time for education. Many of them care for children or hold part-time weekend jobs, and the burden of finding steady childcare and ride shares to accommodate in-person classes can be daunting. CEO Nathan knew that, even if a company program covered the entire cost, he and the HR team needed to help workers source adult-friendly online training options that allowed them to study during the times between taking children to and from school, in the quiet hours after children's bedtimes, on weekends, or even on their bus commute to and from work.

The second hindrance to enrollment had to do with affordability. Even though the company was committed to paying the cost of tuition and books, it did so by reimbursing the workers upon completion of the courses. These adult students were limited in the cash flow needed to carry the up-front expenses until they were paid back by the company. In a sense, the company's seemingly generous education policy was a mirage. The benefit looked good and was there for the employees to use, but, realistically, workers were unable to take advantage of the tuition program—the barriers making it just out of reach.

The vital importance of affordability can never be overestimated. In a May 2020 *Report on the Economic Wellbeing of US Households*, the Federal Reserve found that "[t]he high cost of college was a contributing factor to not continuing or pursuing education for many people. 6 in 10 adults ages 22 to 39 who never went to college or never finished an associate or bachelor's degree cited cost as a reason for their decision."

Nathan told the NSC audience that he decided to do things differently upon receiving the feedback from his workers. First, he and his HR team proactively sought out respected online learning options for his workers that allowed them to move at their own pace and offered greater schedule flexibility. Today, especially since the pandemic, the number of accredited higher education institutions offering adult-friendly formats has grown exponentially.

In addition, Nathan's company restructured the benefit to make affordability within reach of more workers, changing it from tuition reimbursement to tuition disbursement. With the latter, the simple tweak of fronting the money made all the difference in the world. The company subsequently boasted 600+ takers for tuition benefits, up from the original measly 70.

Let's look more deeply into this CEO's playbook.

Learning as a Loop

Why does the story of Nathan's company matter? The future of work will expect organizations to move at the pace of business—or speed of need, as discussed in a prior chapter. This requirement imposes on workers a common set of realities: skills are evolving; workers need to keep up; learning must be continual. You've no doubt heard the term *lifelong learning* floating around. For decades, it was used in the context of staying mentally active, like learning Italian or picking up a new hobby. In recent years, the mention of lifelong or continuous learning has emerged in policy discussions as a strategy for enabling workers to stay relevant and weather rapid workplace changes. In this model, rather than viewing education as a one-and-done deal, frequent skill boosters become the norm and not the exception.

The timing of this semantic shift has coincided with the rise in anxiety levels about the future of work reported in several new books and articles. The World Economic Forum's latest 2020 *Future of Work Report* states, "Automation, in tandem with the COVID-19 recession, is creating a 'double-disruption' scenario for workers."

The McKinsey Global Institute anticipates some 75 million workers worldwide needing to switch occupational categories in the next ten to fifteen years from automation. To help employers facilitate employee transitions and encourage employee participation in ongoing training, the Aspen Institute Future of Work released a toolkit entitled *A Step-by-Step Guide to Evolving to Tuition Disbursement.*

In 2018, Walmart announced a robust tuition support program for their frontline associates—including cashiers and warehouse workers—designed with elements recommended by the Aspen toolkit. I was invited to speak on a panel featuring its launch at the Walmart annual shareholder meeting at the company's headquarters in Bentonville, Arkansas. Within a year's time, *Forbes* reported that more than 7,500 employees from all fifty states had been accepted into higher education through this program to improve their skills, with the company estimating that more than 52,000 Walmart associates would take advantage of the benefits in the first five years. Employees become eligible for the program upon working at least ninety days, and those who leave the company before completing a degree do not have to pay back any costs to Walmart (though their education subsidies will stop).

Walmart is only one in a notable league of corporations who in recent years announced an extension of higher education benefits to entry-level employees—not just managers or high potential staff, as was traditionally the case. Starbucks's College Achievement Plan made Arizona State University degrees accessible to their baristas. Amazon's Career Choice paid 95% of educational benefits—up to an annual maximum—with entry-level fulfillment center employees eligible for the program.

Employers have historically hesitated to invest in employees who may end up finding a job elsewhere. My father-in-law had a successful thirty-seven-year career with the industrial giant Boeing. As an employee, he was trained, rotated into assignments, upskilled, and given challenging projects to enhance his capabilities and expertise. This type of implied "employment compact" where the company invests in an employee with the expectation of long-term loyalty is indeed rare nowadays.

The US Department of Labor estimates that today the average time an employee spends with an employer is less than five years.

Countries such as Singapore have already recognized the transient relationship between workers and employers by facilitating training resources to be portable and available to the worker rather than accessible only through an employer.

In my recent interview with Dr. Soon Joo Gog, chief futurist at SkillsFuture in Singapore's Ministry of Education, for my WorkforceRx podcast, she explained that her country offers a centralized fund to which employers and employees can both contribute monthly. The saved funds can be used by the person at that individual's discretion for training to upskill. Regardless of whether the person is a full- or part-time employee or a gig worker, the dollars move with the individual. The benefit is designed for portability, so how the person chooses to spend the money is uncoupled from any influence of the employer.

The issue of portability as it relates to continual learning is a hot topic that will be covered in greater detail in chapters 8 and 10. For now, I'm concerned about the cost of these training boosters if they are to be done continuously throughout a worker's lifetime. Highlighted in reports issued by the Aspen Institute for the Future of Work and the National Governors Association's *Future Workforce Now* is the conundrum of who pays for continuous learning. The student loan infrastructure is already taxed, hovering at $1.7 trillion in 2021. While the employee can be helped with employer-provided models like tuition disbursement, employee tenure with companies is limited. This leaves the burden on the worker to pay.

A social (or human) infrastructure that could help individuals afford keeping up their skills is a concept of tax-advantaged structures called lifelong learning and training accounts. Workers could use these at any time during their careers to pay for education and training, just as our Singaporean counterparts already do. While the lifelong learning and training account may bear different names, it is essentially designed to travel with the worker, much like our 401(k) retirement contribution accounts that are matchable by employers but stay with us when we change jobs.

The policy is intended to incentivize individuals to save funds that they can tap into over their lifetime and at the same time establish a way for employers to contribute funds. These accounts would be portable, going with individuals as they move from job to job and, similar to the Singaporean program, decisions about how to use the funds would rest with the workers, not employers. As self-employment increases, which includes work through technology platforms, portable benefits such as those in a lifelong learning and training account demonstrate how our social structures are evolving to keep up with the speed of need.

All Things Portable

You've no doubt heard of the concept of portable benefits before. According to the Aspen Institute, benefits—especially healthcare and retirement—are critical to household financial security. Most US workers historically receive benefits coverage through their employers, a method that worked fine when work arrangements lasted decades, not years. In contrast, portable benefits are connected to an individual, rather than to a particular employer, allowing workers to move from job to job or gig to gig without interruption in coverage or, worse, loss of funding altogether.

When it comes to portable benefits, I am not only referring to health or retirement benefits or even lifelong learning and training accounts. Added to this list of portable assets on the frontier of experimentation is the concept of a learner and employment record (LER), also referred to as an interoperable learner record (ILR). While these naming conventions will simplify over the long term into something that will better roll off the tongue, let's use these acronyms for now.

LERs rose in visibility during the Trump White House American Workforce Policy Advisory Board discussion. According to Shalin Jyotishi of the New America Foundation, "These LERs are essentially digital passports where the full breadth of our learning and skills can be brought into one centralized place." If learning is to be continual, the traditional college transcript is too static and narrow to reflect a potential employee's qualifications. What if workers could represent who they are through a comprehensive digital record of all their skills gained through formal schooling, informal and structured training on the job, conference attendance, project performance, volunteering, military service, or other experiences? Can this record better communicate a worker's full scope of skills?

Explains Shalin, "This may seem like a very meta sort of pie-in-the-sky idea, and it is nascent but there is a great deal of momentum under way for LERs."

The T3 Innovation Network uses educational and workforce data to create an open and decentralized public-private data ecosystem to articulate a person's skills, not just list degrees as proxies for competencies. T3 recently came together with the US Chamber of Commerce Foundation to prototype the concept. Their hope is to chart a path forward where learning records can.

Why this type of data consolidation is happening becomes more understandable when we explore its context. At the invitation of Barbara Adachi, president of the International Women's Northern California Forum, I spoke to a Zoom audience of sixty women leaders on the future of work. I asked these successful women how confident they were in giving advice to a teenager about what skillsets will be of value ten years out. Surprisingly, only 10% of this highly educated and professionally successful crowd reported being crystal-ball confident. The informal survey indicated a recognition that jobs and skills are changing rapidly. The World Economic Forum predicts that 42% of core skills will change for workers by 2022.

As Wayne Skipper, the big-hearted technologist and CEO of Concentric Sky whom I happened to meet at an event at the Institute for the Future, would say, "My toddler will likely work in a job that doesn't exist today. How will we know what skills are valued in that future?"

He gave me hope that my teenager's love for video gaming might one day translate into the hand-eye dexterity that tomorrow's robot-assisted surgeon or drone pilot will need. (More on Wayne and his innovative thinking in chapter 8.) All dreaming of an imagined high-tech future aside, one thing we can expect is that artificial intelligence capabilities will be much more mature to help match workers and work. If so, representing the worker through a more comprehensive LER could mean the difference between getting the gig or not.

Apprenticeship as a Learn-and-Earn Model

We've seen how flexibility and affordability play key roles in enabling adult workers to acquire more education. Incentives such as tuition disbursement play an important role in this process. But what about the opportunity for workers to earn a paycheck while they learn?

Apprenticeship is a proven model not only for reliably creating a skilled workforce that allows individuals to receive a salary while they work and train, but also for delivering on inclusive upward mobility. People do not have to trade income in order to attend training. Apprenticeship is a well-established model pervasive in Germany, France, Canada, Australia, England, and other nations. In the US, this workforce development model has received bipartisan support, yet its adoption historically has been limited. My first exposure to Registered Apprenticeship, which is a designation conferred when the training meets national standards for quality and rigor, was through PG&E.

I remember the day I showed up at PG&E's lineman training facility out in Livermore, California, proudly donning a pair of borrowed industrial boots. My job as the head of workforce development for the company meant I needed to have a better understanding of how our operations field talent would be developed once hired. Quite literally, I wanted to know what it was like in these highly skilled workers' boots.

Dan Amour, PG&E's director of training, invited me to witness a demonstration of how maintenance is performed on a live high-voltage power line. (Reader, please don't attempt this at home, as it is extraordinarily dangerous.) Dan had undergone years of apprenticeship training and seasoning as a journeyman to reach master teacher status to be able to perform this technique. By the time I arrived at the facility, he had already submerged a set of thick rubbery gloves into a water bin specially designed to test for holes. One little hole at that voltage is enough to kill.

We both stepped onto a truck with an elevator arm that carried us up twenty feet toward the power line erected in the training field. My knees got weak as we neared the live wires; at this proximity, I could hear the power buzzing back and forth along the line. Dan helped me don my rubber gloves and instructed me to mirror his technique for touching the live power lines. My fight-or-flight instincts would let me touch it only briefly. That fleeting instance near the buzzing line clarified for me how essential it is for the people in these roles to be trained properly and thoroughly; the work allows for no margin of error.

It was an ideal introduction to a Registered Apprenticeship training program that assesses skills with a rigorous set of standards as they climb up a wage scale. The motivation is clear for the worker, who not only earns a base salary but also has the promise of earning raises as they master new techniques. As more skills are added to a worker's competencies, more earning potential is achieved. Once level one is mastered, apprentices proceed to levels two, three, and so on, coinciding with pay increases before arriving at what is called journeyman or a journeywoman status, signifying mastery over all of the competencies needed for a particular trade. The road to journey status usually takes between three and five years.

Not every trainee goes the distance in the apprenticeship program, as Dan will tell you. But those who do are reliably well trained. And, in an industry as long standing as the energy and utility one, those who operate at the journey level find their skills transferable from company to company and state to state. That's the journey element of the job title, and the industry credential they earn is highly portable.

As a matter of fact, during one particularly bad rainstorm with significant power outages, reciprocity was invoked and hundreds of journey workers from neighboring electric utilities in nearby states traveled into California to deliver mutual aid. These highly skilled individuals headed straight to work in the storm to restore downed power lines with no additional training needed. Clearly, at PG&E and other similar companies with high-risk jobs, the investment in upskilling employees in such a methodical way is well worth it since employers are assured of the quality they want from workers who successfully come out of a Registered Apprenticeship program.

The benefits of upskilling need not be limited to behemoth operations. Small companies that lack the resources to create their own apprenticeship programs can easily pool their efforts to create a highly specialized workforce as well. Perhaps two or three of them have a common or similar worker classification that can be a focus of collaboration. Knowing that joining forces in these cases is often a win-win, even large companies opt for a collaborative training approach.

The Education Fund, formed by multiple hospital employers and the labor union SEIU–UHW, is one example of an employer-union-advised training trust in which companies gather and prioritize their training needs and jointly invest resources to take action. If you'd like to research this type of trend further, look for additional examples of training trusts in the building trades and automotive industries.

An important concept in the workforce development world is training contextualization. This concept is especially important for adult learners. Registered Apprenticeships train skills relevant to the job at hand; work is the context for learning those competencies. If you mandate a group of mechanics to take a course in computer basics, chances are they won't see its relevance and will decline registering. That's the experience of Dave Meisel, who headed up the enormous PG&E fleet and staff of over 300 mechanics that I discussed in chapter 1.

Instead, if the same content is embedded into a course on the maintenance of electric vehicles, the story changes. Suddenly, the training becomes relevant, and the mechanic will show up. This is the power of apprenticeship training: every competency in the curriculum is related to the performance of one's job.

Paving the Way toward the Future of Support

Collaboration can take many forms and include a variety of actors. In 2010, I was fortunate enough to help launch the White House initiative that built national awareness of the role of employer-led skills training and the upskilling of workers. At his meeting of the President's Economic Recovery Advisory Board (PERAB), Barack Obama announced Skills for America's Future, an industry-led initiative to dramatically improve industry partnerships with community colleges and build a nationwide network to maximize workforce development strategies, job training programs, and job placement.

I was then still in the private sector with PG&E and led my company's participation with the PERAB Education and Training Subcommittee as well as its involvement in Skills for America's Future. Five companies were featured in the initial launch: PG&E, The Gap, McDonald's, United Technologies, and Accenture. As was outlined in the press release, since "employers identified public/private partnerships as one of the most effective ways to improve the skills and credentials of American workers and students," Skills for America's Future aimed to create platforms to galvanize collaborative action. The participating companies began to recognize their roles in skills development and took powerful first steps to institute tuition support, expand apprenticeship training, and adopt other workforce development strategies to hire more inclusively and grow talent with greater intentionally.

As the 2020 COVID-19 pandemic showed us, even with the best planning, disruptions occur for which no workforce development playbook yet exists. Take a look at the following plan of action created in just fourteen business days to accommodate the speed of need with an impressive display of agility.

The Great Talent Swap

I met Eva Sage-Gavin when she was heading up global human resources for the clothing retail giant The Gap, Inc., and we stood together at the White House to launch Skills for America's Future. It didn't take long for me to see that Eva was a cutting-edge thinker.

Today, she leads a major revenue-generating division of Accenture, a multinational professional services firm, as Senior Managing Director of their Global Talent and Organization/Human Potential Practice. In March 2020, Eva developed a unique and effective approach to handling workers displaced by the COVID-19 pandemic. She, Accenture's CEO Julie Sweet, and a number of chief human resource officers across different industries got together over Zoom to discuss the pandemic-related workforce crisis. Across all their companies, COVID-19 would put some portion of their capable workforce out of work, while other companies actually would grow during the pandemic. They decided they could help address the unemployment crisis.

Within fourteen business days, a platform called People + Work Connect was set up to match employers and talent within a network that would spread to ninety-five countries, with 257 organizations on board in just under a year. On this platform, 130,000 positions were posted, and 270,000 workers positioned themselves to be employed. It was a simple, elegant solution. As the economy changed overnight, similar agile workforce solutions across most industries would need to crystallize just as quickly.

What is memorable about the creation of People + Work Connect is that the employers, while taking action to reduce their workforce as they needed to do, took the compassionate action to allow newly released talent to find another home. I appreciated the stewardship that was implied—placing value on the talent by facilitating their recirculation through employment with others. In this chapter, you also saw stewardship rendered when companies offered tuition support for entry-level workers, especially if the degrees or certif-icates were in programs of study driven by labor market need but not necessarily of benefit to the company directly.

CHAPTER HIGHLIGHTS

- Filling the need for talent means not just hiring well but also developing employees' talent within an organization.
- The two elements that serve as barriers that keep employees away from upskilling programs are issues of flexibility and affordability.
- Tuition support is best implemented as disbursement and not reimbursement.
- Employers are increasingly extending education benefits to entry-level workers, not just to managers.
- It is not enough just to provide resources to workers; we need to make sure those resources actually get used.
- Apprenticeship is a proven model for reliability, creating a skilled workforce that allows individuals to be paid while working and learning. The presence of a paycheck during training can ensure equitable participation.
- Continuous and lifelong learning is essential if employees are to stay current and weather the changes that are affecting all industries. Workers will need additional ways to finance their ongoing upskilling upon being decoupled from the employer.
- Portability of assets is the new infrastructure needed in the future of work. Portable benefits, lifelong learning and training accounts, and learner and employment records represent frontiers of experimentation at national scale.

In this chapter, I talked about flexibility, affordability, and on-the-job training models, all helpful instruments on the tool belt of workforce development. Now let's see how we can scale our practices to effect change even beyond our field of vision.

Five

Forming an Echo Chamber
of Support

CHALLENGE:

How can we scale workforce development
to improve employability and
retention at the same time?

SOLUTION:

Companies and colleges must find
a team of innovators who will
motivate and inspire others.

Over the past decade, the term *echo chamber* has gotten a bad rap from social media critics who have made the concept nearly synonymous with tunnel vision, epistemic bubbles, political polarization, and outright small-mindedness. All but forgotten is the powerful capability of an echo chamber to mobilize and amplify the sentiment of a large group striving to accomplish a noble task. This collective momentum is what I have in mind when I talk about the importance of an echo chamber in creating an agile workforce.

Throughout my career, I've witnessed the power of it firsthand: when key players within an organization harness their voices to solve problems and embrace change, there's no telling what lasting, large-scale impact they can have. How do we formulate a strong echo chamber to advance the workforce agenda? Sometimes it takes just one motivating voice to get started.

My Squeaky-Shoes Moment

Peter Darbee was the CEO at PG&E who brought me there initially as his special assistant before I took on a new role to create the company's PowerPathway initiative. I'd worked with Peter before, straight out of business school. Many years later, he continued to impress me—this time around with his broad vision for the company that set it apart from other players in the industry. He positioned PG&E to be the utility sector's front-runner in fighting climate change, a decision that informed all of the company's innovative choices, such as making our supply chain greener or adopting an electric fleet of vehicles to reduce greenhouse gas, a practice that our competitors later emulated.

Back then, the debate among policy makers hinged on the questions, Is climate change real, and are humans responsible? Peter's resounding answer was, "Yes, the climate is changing, and, yes, humans are responsible. Therefore, we also have a responsibility to mitigate the problem." His radical position (compared with those of his peers) on climate change inexorably filtered into the DNA of the company, and we were all compelled to find new ways to contribute to this unifying agenda.

At first glance, no one would have guessed that Peter, a former Goldman Sachs investment banker and Dartmouth grad, would be a champion of the environment. However, when I first worked with him in a different company as the new hire into a management trainee program, I quickly saw that Peter was the type of person who couldn't help but think about the big issues, like the company's social responsibility to the planet. In fact, it was his ability to look past the normal line of sight, beyond the minutiae of day-to-day business, that enabled him to tackle large problems and scale every project he took on. As a chief financial officer, he oversaw not only the financial function, but also the strategy division, a responsibility usual for the role.

I'll never forget my first aha moment with Peter when we were walking down the hallway during a one-on-one meeting, and the stiff soles of my new shoes started to squeak. Rather than break concentration on what we were discussing, he simply looked down at my wedges and very matter-of-factly stated, "Oh, they're a little noisy, aren't they?" before he continued the conversation, totally nonchalant.

Even though Peter made me feel at ease about the small stuff like squeaky shoes, he never hesitated to give me opportunities to step up to the plate for some very important assignments. I believe he knew that, although the company had an array of capable midlevel leaders who had been there for years, he needed to seed the field with new talent. In fact, I was part of the first bumper crop of an MBA recruitment program that Peter set up to do just that.

One of my earliest projects was to evaluate a proposal that came from a facilities company in the hopes of receiving a pledge of investment. I did the analysis in no time but was suddenly faced with the fact that I had never used the desktop application to prepare the slide deck before. Determined not to let my inexperience deter me, I stayed up through the wee hours of the night to teach myself the software in order to whip the presentation together. In one week's time, I was able to get the analysis on Peter's desk, along with an apology for how long it had taken.

To my surprise, Peter took the deck and sent it with a personal note to the then-CEO, saying, "Look at this work product. Normally, it would take me four weeks to get an answer back, and this new hire got me a definitive recommendation in one week!" I hadn't expected this level of praise for a task I'd struggled to get done. However, as I was learning, Peter's can-do attitude was contagious. He simply would throw an assignment at any of us, no matter how seasoned or green, educated or not, with the same expectation. We had no choice but to give it our best shot.

"Run as fast as you can," he'd often say to me. "I'll pull you back if I have to." These words encouraged me to forge ahead many times in my career, in the face of opposition and self-doubt.

I believe that all of us need a Peter—a leader who sees the bigger possibilities and trusts us to move at our own pace, squeaky shoes and all. I'm sure that if you look back on your own career, you'll find at least one person who believed in you along the way, giving you opportunities to prove what you could do. But for every positive voice, there are always a dozen others, many inside your own head, creating a cacophony of negative self-talk. It's important to remember this internal battle for confidence when developing skills training for people who have lost their confidence while unemployed or who come from underserved communities and already are at a disadvantage. Having grown up in an immigrant family, I myself have faced the many challenges of an uneven playing field.

Building Self-Esteem through Peer Networking

Midway through my undergraduate years at Georgetown University, my parents called to tell me that my father's company was experiencing a downturn that might result in my father being laid off. My sister, who was also in college at the time, received the same phone call. Our parents were preparing us for the possibility of having to pause our studies and come home if their finances suddenly changed. For my parents, the greatest champions of education I've ever known, even to consider pulling their children out of school meant the situation must be serious.

Up until this point, I'd worked hard to earn excellent grades and done everything right, so to speak. And yet, here I was, suddenly wondering what lay ahead for me. Voices of doubt and worry began to enter my mind as I questioned my own self-worth. Luckily, my parents' phone call was a false alarm, and my sister and I were able to finish our studies with no breaks. However, that nervous uncertainty left an indelible impression on me.

Later, in business school, I enrolled in a course that addressed the voices of self-judgment and self-doubt that can hinder people from reaching their fullest potential. The professor taught us to recognize the invisible whisperer who sits on our shoulders and tries to stop us from moving ahead in our careers. You probably have one whispering to you that says things such as I'm not good enough; I'm not smart enough; I'm not really ready.

The rule of thumb in workforce development is that if someone has been out of the workforce for more than six months, they have a significant drop in confidence. As of February 2021, the US Bureau of Labor Statistics reported that more than 4 million people had been unemployed for six months or more, a surge of 3 million over the prior year. NPR reported that 41% of all unemployed people can now be considered "long-term unemployed"—a phrase that describes those not employed for longer than six months—at "levels not seen since the height of the Great Recession." The voices of judgment within these individuals can become debilitating if not tamed and replaced with positive self-talk, especially for someone who has been unsuccessfully seeking a job for six months or longer.

Many, many years later, as vice chancellor of the California Community Colleges, I visited Santa Monica to speak as a guest of the policy think tank, the Milken Institute. Santa Monica's average house price was $999,999 at that time, and this particular audience was affluent compared to others with whom I've spoken. I could tell that my comments pertaining to jobs and the economy resonated well because a long line of audience members formed afterward to speak with me personally.

I was surprised to find well-dressed, clearly educated, middle-aged men and women asking for my help to get back into the workforce. The prior downturn had knocked them out of their jobs, and from story after story, I learned that they each had passed the six-month mark when unemployment starts to take a toll on a person's confidence. I saw their dwindling hope in their faces and heard it in their voices and knew that inspiring confidence was one of the final, though often forgotten, ingredients in the workforce development recipe for agility.

Often, what's needed to boost confidence is only a small amount of networking among peers. Take, for example, recently separated military veterans. My PG&E PowerPathway workforce development experience found that bringing this group together in the comfort of each other's company instantly brought their spirits up. Even though we offered mental health services to help address transition issues unique to those who dedicated years in the service, we found that veterans felt alone upon returning from service, even when married.

The case manager and I, in my PG&E capacity, assumed there might be rivalry among the different divisions of forces, but, as it turns out, the entire group of veterans seemed very grateful to regain the camaraderie of others, regardless of division or ranking, who understood what deployment felt like. Military veterans turned out to be a great talent pool for PG&E. The hires were mature, diverse, trainable, and used to the hierarchical culture of a utility. Moreover, they seemed undaunted within an environment where mistakes with a power line might be a matter of life or death. Restoring their confidence through a well-designed workforce development program facilitated their successful transition back into civilian life.

Building Self-Esteem through Soft-Skills Training

Another way to build employee self-esteem and at the same time improve employability is through soft-skills training, a part of workforce development that is often overlooked, yet always in high demand among employers. In fact, I couldn't count the number of times I've heard company executives on advisory bodies complain about the lack of soft skills among their workers and students. It mattered little whether their complaints were directed at four-year or two-year institutions. The theme was pervasive.

Before I get into a discussion about how to address this skill shortage, let me explain what I mean when I say soft skills. These interpersonal skills come by other names: twenty-first-century skills, essential skills, employability skills, success skills, and so on. These terms tend to refer to the nontechnical skills pertaining to how you work, including how you interact with colleagues, solve problems, and manage your work.

Science, technology, engineering, and math (STEM) careers tend to emphasize the four Cs: communication, collaboration, creativity, and critical thinking. Other industries have a longer roster, adding adaptability or cultural competence to the list. EMSI issued a report in 2019 entitled *Robot-Ready: Human+ Skills for the Future of Work* calling for transferable skills, also developed through a liberal arts education, as an inoculation to counter the changes in the future of work. All industries agree across the board that these qualities are valuable assets for all workers to have.

Based on the repetitive complaints from employers, soft skills are a significant deficit for those entering the workforce with the issue spanning graduates of two- and four-year colleges. As vice chancellor, I wanted to make inroads on these soft skills for our community college students. If we succeeded, we would build student confidence and ability to thrive in a career. Community college students tended to be more diverse than their four-year student counterparts so developing a good playbook could lead to workforce diversity, equity, and inclusion.

Pilot Fatigue and Unlocking Scale

For a pervasive workforce skills gap like this, no one institution can solve the problem on its own. A pilot program on one campus is hardly enough to move the needle. There is a phenomenon called *pilot fatigue*, wherein the momentum fades as time goes by, preventing the success from being adopted more widely. As vice chancellor, my division had the funds to issue a grant to tackle soft skills. But, given the ubiquity of the skills gap, I wanted to design into the grant a mechanism to scale the solution, should it prove successful.

Instead of soliciting a single campus to win the grant, my team and I took a novel approach: we used the grant to source a network of ten community colleges who would work together in a community of practice to find a solution to students' lack of soft skills. We wanted an ecosystem of the willing.

The winning grant went to a network of ten institutions led by grant directors Rajinder Gil and Amy Schulz, who began a program they would eventually scale as the New World of Work: 21st Century Skills, devoted to developing soft skills in community college students. Their process identified these as the top ten industry-advised skills deemed most necessary for employability: adaptability, analysis/solution mindset, collaboration, social diversity awareness, communication, digital fluency, entrepreneurial mindset, empathy, self-awareness, and resilience.

Colleges can be compliance-oriented, instead of innovation-oriented because of their natural aversion to risk, a quality that can be quite demotivating for changemakers like Rajinder and Amy. Unfortunately, as well liked and as deeply committed to their cause as they were, the two were under-appreciated by the home college they worked for. As is often the case, their entrepreneurial efforts were thwarted by the institutional bureaucracy that slowed them down by taking too long to pay invoices and demonstrating other sluggish behavior.

I saw in these two women a commitment to their mission and a passion for their space. I wanted to place them where their voices could be heard and have them start to generate the momentum needed to have a meaningful, large-scale impact. I called Rajinder and Amy "key talents." By investing in these women as key talents serving as entrepreneurs to design a solution to close the gap in soft skills and grow the ecosystem of the willing, I was borrowing from the Silicon Valley model of betting on people. I facilitated their move out of their current college and into one that appreciated their entrepreneurial spirit. Shasta College would give them more fertile ground, so to speak.

As requested by the grant issued by my division of the state chancellor's office, Rajinder and Amy went to work. They not only developed a curriculum well received by colleges and employers but also experimented with digital badging, something never before done in the California Community Colleges. I specifically asked for experimentation in the grant because it was time for the system to adapt the new technology for the benefit of our students.

If you haven't heard of digital badges, they very much are like how the Girl Scouts and Boy Scouts would earn physical badges each time they mastered a new skill. Digital badges would be awarded as community college students demonstrated their mastery in each of New World of Work soft-skills competency.

The initial ten colleges approached the curriculum and digital badging well. The echo chamber began to form: initially among the 10 colleges, then the following year, among 20, then 60. By the time I left the chancellor's office years later, they had reached 85 out of the 116 community colleges in the state. Very few practices had gained the J-curve level of adoption (exponential instead of linear), most flailing after pilot fatigue.

Did I crack the code on how to scale promising practices? It appeared that by being intentional in the design up front, I found a playbook for ushering in large-scale impact. In the ensuing years, I repeated the strategy a few times to verify that this J-curve playbook was repeatable. It was.

Irma Perez-Johnson of the American Institutes for Research solicited my advice, during the pandemic, on how to invest millions of new dollars set aside by her board for workforce development grants to community colleges. They wanted systemic impact, not just another program. I gave them the same recommendation: avoid pilot fatigue and design for scale.

Teaching Elephants to Dance

In comparison to pilot fatigue, many of us who have worked in policy are familiar with another phrase *death by pilot*, which refers to the slow but certain decline of interest in a single idea by wearing out the concept through intentional pilot fatigue. In my experience, it is difficult to extrapolate success in a small-scale pilot unless there is some pre-thinking on how success, if found, can be taken to scale. For example, a small pilot can easily keep track of its data and metrics on an Excel spreadsheet. That method won't scale when involving a network of ten partners, which introduces issues of version control and data quality and administrative access to the records.

I also found that bureaucracies can also use pilots as a way to temper the excitement in a particular idea that it does not share interest. Looking at the process of moving ideas into legislation then implementation, it normally takes one to two years at best to pass legislation (at its fastest), three to five years for funds to be expended and evaluations to be documented, and by then the political and economic landscape has already shifted, stakeholders have lost interest, and you've missed your opportunity to scale. In the private sector, startups must work up front on their exit strategy, whether it's to sell or go public. In the nonprofit and public-policy world, a program that lacks an intentional strategy to go to scale also misses the opportunity to make a systems-level impact.

As vice chancellor, I oversaw a range of workforce initiatives created in legislation, including a $24 million economic development program. After about a year and a half of meetings with its advisory body, the Economic Development Program Advisory Committee (EDPAC), which included ten college CEOs, ten industry representatives and other stakeholders, and diligently poring over labor market analysis and scrutinizing the performance of college initiatives fund by these dollars, I started to wonder why we were putting so much rigor into that relatively small amount when $6 billion was sitting adjacent in the system stockpile. The big monies were distributed not through grants but based on student enrollment and retention. If students attended, colleges got paid through formulas set by the state, but if they dropped out of a program early, they weren't. *Apportionment* is the technical term for how colleges were reimbursed for educating students.

At the time, roughly one-third of all students within the California Community Colleges system were enrolled in career programs, which meant $2 billion of the $6 billion was essentially supporting students in workforce programs. I wondered if I could get even 10% of that $2 billion pot to work more effectively using effective practices, then perhaps $200 million dollars, not just $24 million, would be embracing some of the most effective practices over into the larger system to impact an exponentially larger population of students.

Imagine the $2 billion as a slow-moving elephant. What if we could use the best practices within the $24 million potentially to act as a guiding shepherd dog, teaching that behemoth to operate much more functionally for the benefit of a wider swath of students, more than can be reached through $24 million in grants? This eureka reminded me of how Peter Darbee at PG&E thought big when it came to his company's role in climate change. Let's go reshape the big system rather than act on the margin.

Long story short, I succeeded in reshaping the monies, metrics, and data to alter the behavior of the entire system of California Community Colleges. Workforce went from an afterthought to a policy priority in California. Not only did my effort infuse effective workforce practices more broadly to students affected by the $2 billion in public funds, but the state increased its grant funding to career education programs. My division started with $100 million under administration, and by the time I left two gubernatorial terms later, I oversaw over $1 billion in workforce investments above and beyond what was normally apportioned.

The system experienced an unprecedented level of innovation—thanks to the collaboration, experimentation, and adaptation afforded by the playbooks discussed throughout this book.

Rock Pfotenhaur, a well-respected workforce dean across the system with two decades under his belt within the California Community Colleges, exclaimed, "You've made more difference in five years than others have done their entire career in the system."

Dianne Van Hook, Chancellor of the Santa Clarita Community College District, and one of the longest tenured community college administrators was not initially a fan of the changes coming out of my office at the state chancellor's office, but over the years, she became my biggest champion as she saw the positive changes unfolding to make it easier for the field to do good workforce programming. She wrote me in a letter to cheer on my efforts, "Most people take a decade to do one-fourth of what you have accomplished . . . to change the face of our community colleges, our reputation, and so much more going forward."

Next, we'll take a look at some practical ways we can level the playing field of employability and make career opportunities more reachable.

CHAPTER HIGHLIGHTS

- Every company needs leaders who champion the creation of opportunity and mobility in an inclusive way.
- Forming an echo chamber of support can reshape the system rather than make changes that play on the margin.
- In the nonprofit and public-policy world, a program that lacks an intentional strategy to go to scale also misses the opportunity to make a systems-level impact.
- To facilitate greater adoption of effective practices, avoid pilot fatigue and design for scale.
- Everyone can be affected by self-doubt, but people who spend periods of time unemployed are especially so. We must find ways to help them develop confidence in order to succeed.
- Confidence must be developed along with soft skills in a workforce for a winning combination.

Six

Stacking Credentials to Create On-Ramps and Off-Ramps

CHALLENGE:

How can we extend workforce development
opportunities within the classroom?

SOLUTION:

Colleges can embed industry credentials
into degree programs to improve employability.

My Own Nudge Forward

When I was in middle school, my family moved from Honolulu to Dallas so that my father could redo his medical residency; even though he had practiced as a neurosurgeon in Vietnam, his license did not transfer when we immigrated as is the case for all foreign-trained doctors. In the middle of seventh grade, my English teacher pulled me aside and had me take a special placement exam. I remember her distinctly because of her black hair, big eyes, and fair skin—in my mind, like an older version of Snow White. At the time, I had no idea why I was sitting with her in an empty classroom writing down answers to the battery of questions she was asking out loud. She did not tell me any details of why I needed to take the assessment.

For one of the questions, I was asked to write a sample street address on the front of a pretend envelope. I put my name on the first line, my street address on the second line, the city and state on the third line, and the zip code on the fourth. She looked down with a slightly concerned expression and quietly suggested that zip code belonged on the third, not fourth, line—so that I would not get the answer marked wrong. My teacher's desire to see me live up to my potential and her extra little nudge forward got me placed into advanced classes for which, until then, no one had bothered to consider me. Thanks to that intervention I received early on, I eventually went on take all honors classes and graduate as high school salutatorian and class president from Henry J. Kaiser High School upon our move back to Hawaii.

Warren Wu was our class valedictorian. He went on to MIT, and I joined him on the East Coast at Georgetown University. Looking back, that placement test was my first on-ramp experience. (Though, until this day, I think it ludicrous that writing an address label on four instead of three lines might have caused me to miss my on-ramp. Thank goodness for good teachers.)

In many ways, my academic success wasn't optional. As a first-generation American, I knew I couldn't simply fall back on my parents' couch. They were starting over themselves. I had no choice but to work hard and choose pragmatically when it came to majors and minors in college if I wanted to secure a self-reliant financial future after graduation. The reality for most people today is that the cost of higher education is burdensome. The steep levels of student debt have made employability an issue for students in poignant ways.

On average, tuition at colleges and universities has increased in the past decade by 37%, and net costs (factoring in scholarships and grants) have increased by 24%. According to the Institute for College Access and Success (TICAS), 62% of college seniors who graduated from public and private nonprofit colleges in 2019 had student loan debt and they owed an average of $28,950; average debt for college graduates outpaced inflation over the last fifteen years; for eighteen states, student debt grew at more than double the rate of inflation. Americans owed more than $1.7 trillion in student loans, according to estimates for quarter three 2020, an increase of nearly 4% compared to the same quarter in 2019.

As in my circumstances, students are becoming more and more cognizant of the importance of being work ready when they finish their studies. "Many of our students are first-generation college students with hopes and dreams, who seek economic mobility and paths to family-sustaining jobs," explains Dr. Sunny Cooke, super-intendent and president of the Mira Costa Community College District, who served as co-chair of the California Community Colleges Board of Governors Strong Workforce Task Force.

To carry and pay off high levels of student loans, students will find it wise to factor in employability—moreover, employability in positions with good enough wages to pay bills—in their higher education decisions. Student loan had become burdensome enough by the 2020 presidential elections to enter their policy debates with candidates advocating for "free college" surfacing in the debates. Setting aside current student debt load, how future generations pay for continuous upskilling throughout their lives remains a conundrum given the strained state of public coffers.

The cost of college can be a hindrance to enrollment too. According to the Federal Reserve, "The high cost of college was a contributing factor to not continuing or pursuing education for many people. Six in ten adults ages 22 to 39 who never went to college or never finished an associate or bachelor's degree cited cost as a reason for their decision."

Higher education's perceived value diminished during the pandemic. A 2020 Strada Education Network's Center for Consumer Insights report based on Gallup poll surveys identified that COVID-19 drove increased interest among adults without college degrees to consider additional education—and yet this group simultaneously expressed a loss of confidence in higher education's ability to yield desired benefits.

According to Strada's Senior Vice President Dave Clayton, "The percentage of aspiring adults who strongly believe additional education will be worth the cost has dropped from 37 percent to 18 percent. It's even worse for expectations that additional education will help them get a good job, down from 56 percent a year ago to 24 percent today." Clayton concluded with, "Americans feel a greater need for education's promised upward mobility, but their faith in this promise is shaken."

Chaotic times are the moments that invite reflection.

The Need for a New Higher Education Paradigm

Anxious individuals and families are asking themselves, Is college really worth the cost? With today's disruptive forces such as AI, automation, digitization, and the burgeoning gig economy well under way, the nature of work is being revolutionized at breakneck speed. The path to opportunity, which traditionally led directly through a four-year college has become much more circuitous. Higher education faces a major crisis of reinvention.

This need preexisted the pandemic, with some colleges already experiencing financial difficulties. The report produced by *The Hechinger Report* using federal data showed more than 500 public and nonprofit colleges and universities with signs of financial problems. According to Jon Marcus of *The Hechinger Report*, more than fifty closed or merged in the last five years, with no fewer than eight shuttering or announcing their intent to close since the start of the pandemic. Declining enrollments, rising tuition, escalating cost, and changing demographics are only some of the factors playing into the problem.

When COVID-19 lockdowns kept American students out of the dorms and international students out the country, even unwilling faculty had to go online. This reduced the stigma of online education options. While the students span the continuum from positive to negative experiences, all students got a taste of virtual education, which will inevitably seed changes in consumer preferences forever. Look at what is happening in teleworking and telehealth—both forced into reality by the COVID-19 outbreak and not likely to revert fully. With residential colleges reverting to their pre-pandemic formula for success, others needed to rethink their differentiator as prospective students, who previously did not look beyond their own backyards, now consider options from online venues such as Western Governors University, Arizona State University Online, and Southern New Hampshire University Online. Compared to their campus-first brethren who struggled to maintain enrollments, these online behemoths had their enrollments grow rapidly.

The evolution of how people want to receive their education and training will not stop there. I remember facilitating a discussion on the future of higher education. To provoke thought, I asked the 100-person audience to consider these questions: What would happen if Google entered the higher education market? What about Amazon? Netflix? Their postulations were fascinating. Many wanted their learnings delivered real time and personalized, creating learning moments with the ease of YouTube.

Not surprisingly, most youths will tell you that if they need to learn something, they go online first. One immediate implication is that the long lines to register, pay tuition, buy books, and pick up paperwork may be a vestige of the past. Yet, in a panel of university presidents hosted at the University of Santa Clara, when posed with the question, What are your digital strategies? they would confidently mention their website and social media activities. When the question was reframed instead to probe, What are your strategies in a digital world? college leadership acknowledge how behind the times they are. Again, technology is a tough teacher, even to higher education institutions.

The global post-COVID demand for higher education is expected to grow at a steady rate in the coming decade. By 2030, there will be an estimated increase of almost 120 million students enrolled in higher education, according to the UNESCO Institute of Statistics—2.3 million will be internationally mobile, a factor which leads to over a 50% increase for international student enrollment. With online options better accepted, the stark reality is that the competition is only getting stronger. How do educators, businesses, labor, and policy makers make the most of this moment to reinvent the higher education paradigm? As always, the power of agility and collaborative ecosystems are essential.

The Art of Helping Institutions Evolve

For those who live within higher education—or government for that matter—evolution can be slow. Traditions are long standing. Risk tolerance is low with little perceived reward. Shared governance, where decisions must consult a range of stakeholders before taking root, takes time to ponder. Bolder changes beget controversy. Those outside of higher education and government may wonder if it is even possible for these institutions to adapt. Yes, there is a playbook for ushering these institutions into the ecosystem of the willing. I found peer-to-peer approaches to be an effective strategy to aid otherwise unwilling colleges and public institutions alike to learn about and adopt innovations.

In 2015, the National Skills Coalition awarded a State Workforce and Education Alignment Project (SWEAP) grant supported by funding from Chauncy Lennon, who oversaw JP Morgan Chase's $250 million Skills at Work initiative. California, along with Mississippi, Ohio, and Rhode Island, would be among four states to send teams of policy and decision-makers to learn from each other and create policies to close skill gaps, creating "more equitable, efficient, and aligned state workforce development and education systems."

In my vice chancellor role with the California Community Colleges with responsibility for the system's workforce mission, I would be on the state team to represent the Golden State in the peer-to-peer learning process along with Tim Rainey, who led California's Workforce Development Board, and Patricia de Cos who served as deputy executive director of California's K–12 Board of Education.

This playbook paired state teams to learn from each other, and I was astounded by how well the playbook worked. Not only did all our states eventually evolve our data systems by being in the community of practice, but I would later borrow the same learning technique to "nudge" a set of California state agencies toward action. Specifically, at the point where we were stuck on whether to proceed with a set of reforms, I imported colleagues from Mississippi to inspire and "shame" California into acknowledging that the data system we wanted for our adult education system could be built and that Mississippi had already done so. Mimmo Parisi, executive director of National Strategic Planning and Analysis Research Center (nSPARC) within Mississippi State University, flew into Sacramento to speak to the committee of seven state agencies that I co-chaired and outlined for us the art of the possible.

I had met Mimmo through the SWEAP grant where he was a participant on the Mississippi state team. Mimmo was a very charming Italian-born man with Southern manners. He had married a woman from Mississippi and put down roots in her hometown over twenty years ago. From within nSPARC, he built a smart data system that advised multiple governors on the impact of their intended policies, from childhood education to higher education and workforce. Moreover, his data enabled Mississippi's economic development team to successfully recruit a large auto manufacturer away from a formidable neighboring state. That employer loved how nSPARC ran the numbers and found how the state could educate the technical talent needed by the company in time to start manufacturing. nSPARC calculated throughput of students who could put into production using the three-legged stool of workforce development that they would complete.

I was so inspired by Mimmo's work that I later asked for and was given responsibility, on top of my duties to drive the system's workforce mission, for the data and technology portfolio within the California Community Colleges (more to come in chapter 9).

Jobs for the Future, a national workforce nonprofit, employed the same peer-to-peer learning strategy by importing California (me) to the East Coast to speak with a room of forty stakeholders of the City University of New York (CUNY) system. CUNY repeatedly struggled to align the interests of educators, employers, and philanthropy to deliver workforce programming, and it was my task as the keynote to share what we had pulled off in California. The CUNY system was complex, spanning twenty-five campuses across the city's five boroughs, offering a wide range of undergraduate, graduate, and continuing education opportunities to students of all ages and backgrounds. Yet, upon hearing the story of how California successfully reengineered the collaboration of its institutions, the room acceded that similar changes would be indeed achievable within CUNY, whose smaller footprint is equivalent to a region in California.

It's important to know that institutions can learn as we consider what higher education paradigms can materialize.

Inventing a New Language for Credentials

All the SWEAP state teams converged for their first meeting in Florida. Andy Van Kleunen, the brilliant CEO of the National Skills Coalition and one of the most effective policy thinkers I know on the national skills agenda, introduced our keynote. I have since forgotten the speaker's name but do remember he was Florida's Senate pro tempore (aka pro tem) then and passionate and smart about career education public policies. The pro tem cared about the employability of Floridians. But there were a great many colleges and high schools, and employers told him they could not tell whether a graduate had the competencies they desired. A certificate of the same name completed at one college could have taken the student sixty credits to complete while at another was sixteen credits. The same issue played out similarly across vocational programs in the state's high schools. The Senate pro tem explained that his state eventually standardized on industry-valued credentials with employers having responsibility for setting what is valued by the labor market.

The pandemic introduced uncertainties only highlighting the growing concern for higher education and workers to retain their relevance. According to the World Economic Forum, 40% of core skills would change by 2025. To keep up, we need a new converter and connector of education, competencies, and credentials as more and more adults grow interested in upskilling rather than in acquiring more degrees. Polling from the Strada Education Center for Consumer Insight indicated that adults favored the acquisition of skills over degrees during unsettled times.

Colleges such as Golden Gate University in San Francisco that have effectively served adult learners and diverse populations for over a century are now having to think about new ways to embed industry-valued credentials into their bachelors' programs. As an example, Golden Gate University added an undergraduate six-course certificate in Facebook Digital Marketing to give students hands-on experience with online publicity tools such as Facebook Ads, Google Ads, Mailchimp, and more. Students would graduate with not only their undergraduate degree but also an industry-valued credential. This curricular design strategy aids students in being employable.

More astounding is the recent development whereby liberal arts colleges have begun to embed career education into their curricula.

According to *The Hechinger Report,* liberal arts–focused Sacred Heart University in Connecticut launched an Advanced Craft Beverage Brewing course to give students vocational credentials for the state's job market, which boasts 115 breweries. Clarke University in Iowa and Stonehill College in Massachusetts also join the list of liberal arts colleges adding career education options, according to the same article. Small colleges, seeing the number of high school students beginning to plateau and then diminish, want to ready themselves for the competition for enrollment.

According to the Western Interstate Commission for Higher Education (WICHE) report entitled *Knocking at the College Door,* the nation should expect successively smaller annual volumes of high school graduates in virtually every graduating class between 2026 and 2037, and so colleges must reinvent themselves in the hope of appealing to more adults as a way to capture enrollment. "Americans appear to like the idea of embedding career and technical education into academic degree programs," according to Jon Marcus of *The Hechinger Report.*

As higher education evolves to consider employability in its paradigm, doing so does not necessarily diminish the liberal arts focus. Instead, the industry credential can be considered as akin to a minor. While students can still major in English, having a minor in cybersecurity will likely improve their chances of employment. A survey conducted by University Partners and Quest Research of 2,000 adults, when given the choice of hiring an English major, an English major with cybersecurity credential, or an employee with a bachelor's in cybersecurity, respondents were four times more likely to say they'd hire an English major with a credential in cyberse-curity than an English major without one. An industry-recognized credential attached to a liberal arts major distinguished the graduate.

Putting Third-Party Credentials to Work

Around 2013, Steve Wright, who served as statewide director for the information communications technology (ICT) industry within the California Community Colleges, approached the global temp agency Manpower to understand what they heard from clients. Manpower pointed him to the 200,000+ jobs available for office professionals in California each year.

What if the community colleges could create a Business Infor-mation Worker certificate focused on skillsets needed for the typical office worker? Included in this Manpower-endorsed program were basic administrative skills and proficiencies such as Microsoft Office Suite and fundamentals in customer service that have become office staples.

When graduates with this certificate attended the annual campus career fair, Steve was astounded by how well they were received. Instead of eliciting the normal four or five students being invited for interviews as he was used to, employers sought out 120+ students by the end of the event. Apparently, the brand-new Business Infor-mation Worker certificate was a draw for employers.

What started in one community college has now been replicated region-by-region across over most of the system's 116 institutions. As of March 2021, an estimated 108,752 community college students engaged with this curriculum across California with attention to the 278,700 forecasted open jobs.

Industry-valued credentials are a simple solution to help potential employers determine if students have the desired skillsets. Futuro Health adapted Steve's playbook to design a Health IT Specialist program for adults to transition into healthcare. To increase student employability, my team took advantage of the preexisting Google IT Support Professional Certificate, which was valued by industry for roles like end-user support and computer helpdesk support. On its own, it was insufficient for the healthcare setting, so Futuro Health worked with Coursera and Johns Hopkins University to create a course to give IT students context for how these skills are deployed in healthcare work settings, whether in hospitals or clinics. And students became sensitized to privacy issues pervasive in the provision of care.

Futuro Health also added a soft-skills course to round out students' customer service skills. This act of unbundling and rebundling education coursework creates options for students to gain new skills or freshen skills in agile ways not afforded by degrees.

Stackable Credentials

Jim Caldwell, the statewide director for the energy and utility industry sector within the California Community Colleges, devoted many years to building an advisory body of companies and trade associations interested in addressing workforce development. Organizations like the Building Owners and Managers Association (BOMA) and the International Facilities Management Association (IFMA) had shared with him their concerns for finding a qualified workforce. He brought them all together into a statewide advisory body and tasked them with evaluating and selecting which industry credentials were most in demand by their company members.

Their number one choice was the HVAC/R (heating, ventilation, air conditioning, and refrigeration) certificate awarded by the North American Technician Excellence (NATE), the nation's largest nonprofit certification organization for heating, ventilation, air conditioning, and refrigeration technicians. Jim took the credential to the community colleges in Southern California with programs of studies in this field and offered to evaluate their existing curricula to see how well they aligned with the industry's HVAR certificate. The results were eye-opening, to say the least.

Out of the five categories of competencies within the credential, all of the participating colleges had a gap in at least one area, which faculty agreed to fill in. Subsequently, faculty agreed to use the HVAR credential as the common denominator on which they could then build more advanced training in specialty fields. The addition of stackable credentials was easily built on top of the fundamentals, creating a win-win-win situation of fuller enrollment and more options for students to enter varying sub-fields, and employers who were pleased to have standardized skillsets they could rely on.

In this sense, the HVAR certificate was an instant converter for upping students' skillsets and catalyzed collaboration among educators. Rather than competing with one another to attract students, the community colleges combined horsepower to jointly market their programs, creating common promotions to generate enrollment— something they had previously lacked the bandwidth to do alone. Up until this point, faculty members had been overextended; but now, working collectively, they grew overall enrollment.

The momentum generated by these workforce programs operating under a coordinated and collaborative hood created better education options for students. Simply by reorganizing and restructuring to work in an ecosystem of the willing, institutions were able to enroll more students, add more specialty coursework on top of the industry-valued credential, and better meet the needs of the local and regional economy.

Steps toward Regional Collaboration

Once the community colleges started collaborating, it opened the door for larger scale opportunities with employers. Regional industry organizations started to reorganize themselves as well to connect groups of employers with groups of community colleges in a marketplace to match needs and wants.

Trusted neutral entities surfaced to mediate efficient conversations between the educational institutions and employers. These intermediaries, or what we tend to call the neutral brokers, were specific to each region. In the counties of San Bernardino and Riverside, the neutral broker is the Inland Empire Economic Partnership led by Paul Granillo, who trained as a priest but found his calling in facilitating the economic development of a region of California with the lowest higher education attainment rate in the country.

In Central Valley, Deborah Nankivell led the Fresno Business Council to consider its role not only in taking from but also in giving back to the community in stewardship. Valley Vision, under Bill Mueller, was the trusted convener in the Greater Sacramento region despite the proliferation of organizations near the state capital. Bill Allen and Lucy Dunn were leaders of the Los Angeles Economic Development Corporation and Orange County Business Council, respectively.

The Bay Area Council in San Francisco and the Silicon Valley Leadership Group in San Jose were nationally known entities. All these organizations and more, coincidentally, were members of the California Stewardship Network, a network created by former State Senator Becky Morgan who had a vision that regions would be the unit of common action for California. She was right. Regions were more agile.

These trusted neutral brokers worked with me while I was vice chancellor of the California Community Colleges to put into place the Strong Workforce Program legislation to address those issues so that the institutions could produce one more industry-valued credential. With the assistance of the policy organization California Forward led by James Mayer, what resulted in 2016 would be the addition of $200 million in ongoing funds per year ($1 billion over five years) by the legislature and governor to invest in expanding workforce programs that produced skilled workers to fuel regional economies.

The Future of Unbundling and Rebundling of Education

Before the pandemic, students were already struggling with the financial burden of higher education, often choosing whatever local institutions were most affordable or offered the most financial aid. But in 2020, when colleges were forced to go online to stay afloat, geographical barriers that once kept many students fenced into their backyards, so to speak, were suddenly psychologically lifted. Given the combination of online learning gaining mainstream acceptance and consumer preferences evolving, I expect to see over time more and more unbundling and rebundling, as students seek out and combine what they need from higher education.

If an English major can't access a cybersecurity credential at their own campus, why not go online to find it? Allowing students to personalize their education beyond just majors and minors—to include industry-valued credentials—puts unprecedented agility into education at a time when graduates must keep pace with the speed of need.

Holly Zanville of the Lumina Foundation and I co-wrote an article published in *EvoLLLution* observing that "unbundling and rebundling is the approach to build an adult-friendly higher education experience." Because the pandemic decoupled dorms, sports, in-person instruction, socialization, tuition, and other elements of the college experience from the learning itself, it created the space to reimagine how the future of learning will reassemble its component parts, especially for adults.

In the article, we asked, "Can we rebundle higher education in better ways to ready adults for the future of work? Can learning systems reassemble to enable continuous and lifelong learning that keeps pace with the unrelenting rate of change?" We further wrote:

> The prescription for change is clear: unbundle the curriculum, pull content from multiple disciplines (or providers), and rebuild content into smaller learning chunks—more short-term credentials. Couple the curriculum with other elements important in the student

journey, such as financial and student supports. Now
is the time for education providers to do that work, to
assess their individual building blocks and look for ways
to recombine them in order to improve the learning
system for adults. Preliminary findings strongly support
the idea of bundling learning into stackable credentials
to help adults keep pace with the rate of change.

The race for relevance and the pressure on employability is
provoking experiments to modularize the consumption of higher
education in units smaller than the degree. For example, Western
Governors University created its first-ever one-year certificate
when it offered a Medical Assistant Program in 2020. In 2021,
the university broke down the component pieces of its preexisting
bachelor of science in Health Services Coordination into a set of
nondegree certificates, each indexed to immediate employment
opportunities. And, in the curricular redesign, students who earn
those certificates could on-ramp back at a later time in life if they
wanted to pursue more education, with every certificate stacking
into the degree.

Stackability is particularly meaningful for adults who are reticent
to start from scratch. According to the Council for Adult and Experi-
ential Learning (CAEL), adults are two and a half times more likely
to complete a degree if they start with some credits under their belt.

CHAPTER HIGHLIGHTS

- Rising student debt load has shifted student focus onto employability and eroded confidence in families that higher education is worth the cost.

- Higher education institutions, facing a crisis of reinvention to satisfy shifting consumer preferences and changing demographics, are experimenting with reshaping curriculum to allow more on-ramp and off-ramp options.

- Embedding industry-valued credentials into degree pathways can give young students an advantage when competing for their first job out of college.

- Modularization and stackability, always constructed with an eye toward what skillsets are valued by employers, are key themes in instruction and also appeal to adult students.

- Credentials can be stacked to create more enrollment, employability, and, in turn, skilled workers, while also making the educational process more digestible.

- Intermediaries, who serve as trusted neutral brokers, can more efficiently facilitate collaboration among a multitude of education partners and employers.

- A peer-to-peer playbook helps bring reluctant colleges into the future through a form of constructive peer pressure.

Seven

Leveling the Slope of
Unconscious Bias

CHALLENGE:

How do we stop pitting diversity
against workforce quality?

SOLUTION:

Corporations and government must work
with community organizations to
integrate recruitment, screening,
and training for day-one readiness.

The vernacular that has risen up around issues of unconscious bias can itself seem complicated. Recently, on my WorkforceRx podcast, I interviewed Marsha Sampson Johnson, a leading diversity advocate, veteran corporate leader, and longtime friend of mine, and teased out some of this lingo. According to Marsha, diversity is "everything that is different and sometimes common about us across the entire human continuum." Inclusion, she asserts, means "I'm going to make sure I make allowances in my environment for these differences."

As you'll see in a moment from her own personal experiences as a woman of color, Marsha's approach to diversity, equity, and inclusion (DEI) is always proactive and heartfelt.

I first met Marsha over twenty years ago when we were both members of a midcareer executive development fellows program run by the International Women's Forum (IWF). As one of the youngest in my cohort of fourteen up-and-coming executives from both the private and nonprofit sectors, I felt honored to be counted among such accomplished women as Marsha, who had decades of leadership in corporate management, HR, talent management, and diversity under her belt. Throughout the years, my respect for Marsha has only deepened as we have gotten to know each other on a more personal level. One poignant story she told me brings the issue of diversity home to such a point that I thought I'd share it here.

A few years ago, when Marsha's sister passed away, her sister's thirteen-year-old grandson came to live with her. Daily postings on the Nextdoor app warned about sightings of "suspicious looking" young Black men in the neighborhood, equating "suspicious" and

"Black." Marsha, aware of the unfortunate but very real possibility that some of the residents in her predominantly White neighborhood may mistake this young stranger as a perpetrator, took a forward approach to preempt any potentially hostile or, worse, tragic outcomes.

Before her nephew moved in, she went door-to-door, handing out over sixty flyers with his photo and name, along with her address, introducing her neighbors to him. It was a straightforward move and, sadly, a necessary one in light of recent tragic news stories. As I listened to Marsha's story, I realized that I never had to worry for my mixed-race sons to the same degree. I know her grand-nephew remains uncomfortable jogging or taking a walk in the neighborhood that is now his home.

Marsha has always taken a holistic approach to DEI in the workplace. On companies' efforts to provide inclusive hiring and retention practices, she has this to say: "Diversity and inclusion can never just be a program. It can never be a department. If it is not incorporated into every aspect of the organization, it will never be successful."

According to Marsha, only once we've achieved equity by leveling the playing field can we truly have inclusion. Otherwise, she explains, "We get the onesies and the twosies . . . we continue to make exceptions. So, we have what we call the token diverse person representing whatever group you want to name, or whatever characteristic you want to name, but it is only through having accessible systems and creating an equitable platform that we can end up with an inclusive environment." Marsha is right. The question for all of us remains: just how do we level the playing field?

The Three-legged Stool to Support DEI at all Levels

In chapter 1, I described the foundation of workforce development as a three-legged stool of collaboration among employers, community organizations, and education providers, with each entity doing what it does best. The collective method reliably generates an inclusive talent pool with the right skills at the right time. This process is generalizable to other arenas to create an equitable playing field.

For example, how do you give smaller businesses a leg up, so to speak, to be able to compete with the larger incumbent suppliers? How do you give disadvantaged communities a chance to be competitive for resources? Designing the competition in an equitable fashion is no easy feat. In my work as vice chancellor, I found time and again that the better-resourced community colleges always won the big state competitions because of their ability to retain grant writers to build relationships, attend webinars, and submit top-quality proposals every time. Running these grant programs in the traditional way never gave the smaller institutions from predictable zip codes even the hope of a chance because of this built-in bias.

However, by pairing well-resourced colleges with those less endowed (I refer to not just financial resources but also staff acumen), we were able to level the playing field. Take, for example the San Diego region of a highly resourced conglomerate of community colleges that sits next door to the Imperial Valley whose economics could not be more different. This latter region, in fact, lagged so poorly in capacity that historically, even when a grant was offered, the monies actually were returned by the community college because the institution lacked the managerial capacity to do the work.

The thought of having to return free money may seem ludicrous to some. To me, the college's inability to execute these grants indicated an unconscious bias. As a steward of public monies, I continually found myself having to strike a balance between allocating funds where grantees who were sure to handle them with the greatest finesse would surely win them and the need for diversity, equity, and inclusion.

I decided to pilot a model where the money could go to a San Diego community college as fiscal agent under the condition they provide the technical assistance to their struggling neighbor. San Diego's comparatively extensive experience running workforce development programs, which included handling all of the paperwork that goes into executing grants, was the exact ingredient that Imperial Valley needed to be up and running at the same level as its sister schools. And by making San Diego the lead applicants to these grants, that region would receive enough percentage of the monies to reap their own benefits as well.

True to the three-legged stool model, by allowing an entity to do what it did best, in this case, grant writing and handling the nuts and bolts of accounting for grants management, the situation pivoted into yet another win-win within the ecosystem of the willing.

Building Confidence and Collaboration Among Peers

In my role as vice chancellor, I saw that a number of our rural colleges seriously lagged in their understanding of workforce development. As a strategy co-designed with the American Association for Community Colleges to build their capacity, my team retained Jim Jacobs, the well-regarded, retired president of Macomb

Community College out of Michigan with a strong national reputation in workforce development, and assigned him as coach to six
of these struggling colleges. In doing this, we were able to build
the wherewithal among these rural institutions. A small amount
of training in the basics such as how to have conversations with
potential employers, how to identify a company's labor needs, and
how to internally respond to these needs went a very long way in
boosting the confidence of these colleges' workforce development
officers. Jim could have taught a master class and, in his retirement,
loaned much-needed tutelage to nudge the rural colleges along.
After six months, Jim observed that most of those he coached had
no one else locally to turn to for advice.

As I mentioned in chapter 5, many of us have an invisible
whisperer sitting on our shoulders, acting as the voice of doubt.
Among our lower-resourced community colleges, those voices
can be multiplied a hundred times over, resulting in a silent but
powerful cacophony of self-criticism and defeat. As employers,
workforce development professionals, public-policy makers, and
educators, a large though overlooked part of our work is to raise a
confident next generation of leaders. Part of doing this is creating
a collaborative playing field.

I always say, "Public needs to get married to public before they
can start courting private." Since the public workforce system is
funded at a federal level yet administered by a vast number of local
agencies, inherent competition and disagreement can arise that deters
industry leaders from getting involved with the possible burden of
having to negotiate between the two entities. However, when the

public is organized and cooperative within its own ecosystem of the willing, it will attract the private-sector players.

Removing Disadvantage through Intentionality

Dr. Sunita Mutha, the director of the Healthcare Center at the University of California San Francisco and a recognized expert in culturally competent care, has focused her research on the intersection between quality improvement and healthcare disparities. Sunita believes that if healthcare providers always asked themselves the following question, healthcare disparities based on race, income, and other factors would be reduced: "Whom does this advantage, and whom does it disadvantage?"

On a recent episode of my WorkforceRx podcast, she provoked thinking by offering examples of practices used by healthcare providers that automatically rule out certain parts of the community, creating built-in inequalities. "You could have predicted whom you'd leave out," she asserts, "by the strategies you choose to use." The exclusive use of telehealth, for example, rules out potential customers who have no internet access or computers at home.

While Sunita's experience is with healthcare, the same principle applies to higher education. Jamie Merisotis, author of *Human Work in the Age of Smart Machines* and another recent guest on WorkforceRx podcast, is a well-known proponent of experimentation to level the slope of unconscious bias. He recognizes the fact that for students at community colleges, nontuition expenses are only about 80% of the total cost of attendance that can prevent enrollment and graduation. He says, "We know that if you can adequately address the combination of factors like childcare, transportation, food, and housing, you can increase completion rates by 10% or more. And then if you add things like advising and other forms of holistic support, so that it's not piecemeal, you can get to even higher levels of success."

I have found that the key to erasing these unconscious disadvantages is practicing intentional intervention. At Futuro Health, one of our tuition-free training offerings was undersubscribed, so we decided to do a spot campaign to beef up awareness and enrollment. We also wanted to make sure that California's significant Latino population of 39% was represented, so we decided to retain a Latino-run PR firm, who executed a set of Spanish radio ads and used Spanish social media influencers to get the word out. The firm advised us that their community responds better to videos than to text, particularly visuals that featured people who were Latino themselves.

Listening to this advice, we recruited several of our Latino students to create video testimonies of their experience with Futuro Health. We also learned that the Latino community prefers talking on the phone to a live representative who speaks their language rather than interacting more efficaciously through a website. So, Futuro Health set up a bilingual landing page with videos peppered throughout and a bilingual call center. Before the campaign, enrollment had been in the twenties. By the time we were done, about 700 people had expressed interest in the English Readiness for Allied Health course.

Many moons ago, I remember a meeting of a local workforce board, where staff were stymied by the low numbers representing diverse communities. When I asked when they held the training, I discovered that it was weekday afternoons. I observed to the others gathered around the table the fact that many of the clients who need the service had jobs and, therefore, would only be available on the weekends or in the evenings. A quick change of the program's time of day yielded powerful results, when, a month later, the same staff member came to report full enrollment.

Similarly, many large companies that post jobs have such an influx of applicants that they make it a regular practice to open the application window for a limited time period. PG&E, for example, posted some jobs only for one hour because, if they were to leave the window open longer, the system would get flooded with applications and the HR team lacked the personnel to sort through the volume. I understood the HR rationale. But how would an outsider, that is, someone who is neither friend nor family to the company's existing employees, even know about this flash posting? This was another small example of unconscious actions that prevent inclusion.

Looking Past Keywords in the Talent Search

Part of the PG&E PowerPathway workforce development strategy to combat unconscious bias was to apply collective action in the model of the three-legged stool. When the company ventured on its own previously to source diversity, it found disappointment when only one out of thirty applicants could pass the preemployment written test. By establishing relationships with specific community organizations to outreach, screen, and case manage and by collaborating with education providers to train, the company successfully grew a qualified and diverse talent pool, as is the promise of the three-legged stool.

In the final step, when it came time for graduates to apply for jobs, we offered what's called a community benefits commitment. This wasn't a guarantee of job acceptance by any means; we instead pledged first consideration of those who came through PowerPathway-branded programs. Community benefits clauses are often incorporated into big public construction contracts as a way to ensure some fraction of the entry-level jobs generated by the project would go to local candidates. These clauses represent a public-policy tool for job creation.

Another type of bias in many companies' hiring processes lives in the computerized applicant tracking system, which goes solely by keywords gleaned from applicants' resumes, leaving out any human judgment. I remember a PG&E frontline supervisor recounting leaders in the company whom he'd hired despite their not having all the right pedigrees; rather, he was impressed with their attitude or drive and wanted to give them a chance in entry-level roles. With the applicant tracking system in place, those young men would now be invisible to this supervisor. Given this type of technology setup, perfectly qualified candidates can be overlooked merely because they did not meet the parameters of the keyword search.

Part of the PowerPathway program's success lay in our community benefits commitment: this meant we instructed graduates what keywords to enter into their online profile and conversely instructed HR to search for those exact same terminologies in order to give first consideration to applicants cultivated through the three-legged stool method of workforce development.

I feel compelled to share my fish story. In running the Pow-erPathway program, my team and I got to know candidates on a personal level, apart from logarithmic calculations and keyword metrics. One such young man left an indelible impression on our team. At nineteen, Aleki was vibrant in personality and had the physical prowess requisite for the job. He grew up in a nearby minority community. My PG&E colleagues and I thought he'd be the perfect fit for the company and couldn't wait to see him on the shortlist of applicants to pass the preemployment steps that included the physical and written tests, the drug test, and the background check. So when Aleki disappeared from the shortlist, I couldn't help but ask the case manager to dissect what had happened.

After some investigation, she discovered that Aleki hadn't passed the background check due to an unpaid ticket he'd received at age fifteen for having caught and kept a fish that was too small by regulation standards. The ticket had escalated when he didn't pay the fine and was sent to the courts. He, unwittingly, by not showing up, became charged with a nonviolent felony that effectively excluded him from most jobs in the energy utility sector for which he'd been trained. Aleki had no idea there was a felony on his record. Yet, the felony surfaced during the PG&E background check and precluded Aleki from employment.

While the circumstances surrounding Aleki's case were unfor-tunate, the most devastating part for me was the fact that, had my team not taken the time to look into the reason behind his rejection, this talented, hardworking individual would have fallen through the cracks of the system. Not only would he have missed the opportunity to work at PG&E, Aleki would never have known, during attempt after attempt, the reasons for his rejection that had nothing to do with his qualifications or readiness for a job. Most companies don't take the extra step as we did to let the applicant know what happened. Instead, they would merely send a notice saying thank you, but you are no longer being considered for the job.

Luckily, since my company was committed to workforce development, the case manager worked with Aleki to get his record expunged, and we hired him. I tell this fish story to help us appreciate how easy it is to become a sidelined talent.

A similar case arose a few months later with Dimitrua, a capable, friendly young woman whose warm smile came across even on the phone. She came to work at PG&E as a temporary worker in the role of my assistant. Fast-forward two years, when I finally had a headcount available to hire her as a full-time worker, Dimitrua passed every test except her background check.

Because I knew her skills firsthand and that she had been performing well in the role, I looked into the situation and discovered that, many years back, she had refused to pay a parking ticket she deemed as unfair. Her unwillingness to pay had left a black mark on her record that disqualified her from being hired, according to company policy.

After many conversations, I finally persuaded Dimitrua to swallow her pride, dip into her bank account, and pay off the ticket, which had since ballooned to cost $600. Once she did so, I hired her into a full-time role with a good salary and benefits. She stayed at the company years beyond my tenure there and aptly performed her job.

Both Aleki's and Dimitura's situations made me wonder whether the failure to return a fish-too-small or a parking ticket—neither actions were related to the jobs at hand—were just in affecting someone's ability to get a job they had the skills to do.

To probe into this question on whether we perhaps were unconsciously sidelining talent, I invited onto my WorkforceRx podcast Byron Auguste, CEO of Opportunity@Work. He was a management consulting partner with McKinsey & Company when I first met him and later became an Obama appointee to the National Economic Council.

Byron outlined for me why skills-based hiring is preferable over degree-based hiring to reduce bias: "When it comes to American workers twenty-five and older, around 40 percent of them have bachelor's degrees. So, if those degrees are a prerequisite for a job, we are saying more than 60 percent of adult Americans are not allowed to compete for those jobs. That requirement immediately rules out 76 percent of African Americans, 83 percent of Latinos, and 81 percent of rural Americans. It says to them that no matter what skills they have, they can't be considered for a position."

Byron pointed to the overlooked talent pool of 70 million Americans who have a high school degree or equivalent, but not a four-year degree—a group he calls STARs or workers who are Skilled Through Alternative Routes. STARs typically gained their skills through a mix of on-the-job learning and experience, military service, community college, and workforce training programs. Rather than use the degree as an automatic screen out of candidates, Byron posits that employing skills-based hiring acts as a more inclusive talent practice. He argues, if you can do the job, you should get the job.

In recent years, several institutions have made great strides in thinking through the many ways implicit bias can infiltrate the hiring process. As part of his work as the director of the Center for Workforce and Economic Opportunity at the Federal Reserve Bank of Atlanta, Stuart Andreason tracks trends in the economy to determine what skills workers and businesses need to be successful. I recently spoke with Stuart on WorkforceRx, the podcast, about the growing need for experimentation in all areas of workforce development, from tuition assistance to skills-based hiring practices. Stuart's bold advice to educators and industry leaders is this: "I would say, 'Try one new thing.' The worst that can happen is that we learn from it and try something different next time."

As we will see in the next chapter, by approaching ongoing learning with this same experimental spirit, educators will be able to mobilize the next generation of workers to keep up with the speed of need.

CHAPTER HIGHLIGHTS

- Unconscious bias can predictably advantage some and disadvantage others.

- Diversity, equity, and inclusion practices must be designed into the human infrastructure of organizations to truly level the playing field.

- It matters how the rules of competition are set in determining whether some always win while others always lose.

- Coaching and technical assistance can build confidence to reduce an apparent disadvantage.

- Practicing intentional interventions can level the slope of unconscious bias.

- Be aware of bias built into the use of certain technologies.

- For some jobs, skills-based hiring can offer a more inclusive process than using degrees as a screen.

Eight

Making Education Upgrades
the New Norm

CHALLENGE:

How can skills keep up with the
rate of technology change?

SOLUTION:

Workers should get their highest level
of education up front and assume a
new norm of acquiring ongoing new skills.

The New Meritocracy

Once upon a time, I was invited to a set of meetings at a global software company in Washington State to take a peek at several of their futuristic ventures. Mind-blowing new technologies in augmented reality and virtual reality (AR/VR) were among the many projects discussed as well as a wondrous AI product that scanned for emerging skill patterns undetectable by humans.

My host was particularly excited to show off the AI's early learning and asked the lead data scientist to show me the resulting reports being generated. The PhD leading the AI project looked at me apologetically and explained, "I would love to show it to you, Van, but today the AI is having its designated learning day." His answer mystified me at first, so I asked him to explain further. Apparently, in the race that pits machines against machines, the company's AI system must routinely spend three days each week in the act of "learning"—acquiring data to refine its algorithm.

I had to mentally pause to fully appreciate the moment. If the machines were setting aside this length of time to build their knowledge in order to gain an advantage, I couldn't help but wonder what we humans should be doing to keep ourselves up-to-date. Unlike many critics who see humans as competing against robots in the ever-increasingly competitive labor market, I consider the two players co-inhabitants of a largely adaptable ecosystem: humans and machine. If we are to work side-by-side with them, then we must also adopt ongoing upskilling practices.

For years, people have perceived the rapid advance of work technologies as a threat. But even as everyone fretted about how we humans would keep up with the machine, Jamie Merisotis stayed calm. Pre-pandemic, the level of attention paid to the future of work was high, and so was the anxiety about the question of whether robots would take over human jobs. I interviewed Jamie, CEO of the national Lumina Foundation, in my WorkforceRx podcast, and titled his episode, "The Robot Zombie Apocalypse Is Not Coming," which is a phrase he often employs. Jamie explained:

> Every meeting that I went to for several years was fixated on this robot zombie apocalypse, and I think that we know from history that technology both creates and destroys jobs, and we don't know what will happen this time around. But I do think we should be more interested in the work that humans can do, because I think that is clearly something we can control by better preparing people for that human work. We know what machines are good at. They're good at a lot of things: speed, pattern, algorithms, repetition. But as Ken Goldberg, who runs a robotics program at Berkeley, pointed out to me, machines can't understand subtlety and nuance and how people react in unpredictable ways. So, the more we interact, the way you and I are doing now as humans, the less likely it can be done by machines. What we've got to do is nurture those foundational human capabilities to prepare people for human work and prepare people with the compassion, the empathy, the ethics, the collaboration, the interpersonal communication,

the creativity—traits and characteristics that you don't just innately possess, you also have to develop over the course of your entire lifetime.

Jamie went on to talk about collaborative robots or co-bots who work side-by-side with humans, sharing the same space and have become integral to the new human work experience. Today's digital natives among the millennials and Gen-Zers of our society have grown up with YouTube tutorials and Khan Academy that make being an autodidact almost a birthright. Some would say they have already entered a symbiotic relationship with their devices and would welcome a co-bot world. Often, in a matter of fifteen minutes or less, a skills gap can be closed by just a few clicks on a smartphone. However, for the older Gen-Xers and boomers who came before the internet, creating a norm of educational upgrading does come with its challenges. The stigma of adult learning can be a hindrance in itself since it challenges the obsolescent idea that the more years a person clocks at a job, the more secure and respected they are. A fifty-year-old returning to the classroom after two decades of experience can feel humiliated.

I have an awkward story to share. Only a decade after finishing graduate school, I decided to tiptoe back into the world of education and enrolled in a doctoral program at the University of San Francisco. I proudly prepared for my first day of class by laying aside a backpack, pens, and a new notebook. These were the standard supplies that had enabled my prior academic success. In my doctoral program would be a mix of educators who worked full-time jobs and younger students who came straight from their undergraduate education. On the first day of class, when I pulled out my notebook to take notes from the lecture, the younger students did too, but theirs were Mac notebooks. What a difference a decade made. The younger students had gone straight to digital. Technology is a tough teacher.

In today's gig economy, things count that did not matter before, such as one's personal brand and influencer score. A client's ability to influence your satisfaction scores on a platform such as Upwork has become the all-important factor on which many gig workers' success is hinged. This new meritocracy of work requires a different kind of agility if workers are to keep up with the changing times.

The Agility of Open Standards

Dave Meisel, who formerly headed up the enormous fleet of PG&E, used to speak about the decreasing shelf life of skills within the automotive industry. Years ago, he explained, a technological breakthrough in combustion engines would reign for thirty years before a new one took its place. This type of technological longevity offered a long stretch for skills acquisition, training lead time, and eventual mastery.

Since then, however, the cycle of innovation has gotten shorter and shorter, forcing mechanics to learn at a much faster rate. The electric vehicle, in his example, stood center-stage for over a dozen years before fuel-cell technology sauntered into the limelight. And new technologies continue to arrive at breakthrough speeds. The curtailing effects of skills development at such a rapid clip give workers very little time, making it a greater challenge for them to keep up than it was for their counterparts just two decades ago. The constant technological evolution in certain industries could make it feel as if the reset button is being hit again and again, leveling the playing field each time, as workers, regardless of years on the job, must upgrade their skillsets to stay relevant.

The very act of searching for work has seen several different iterations over the past few decades. Workers of my generation most likely found their first few jobs in the classified ads of their local or national newspaper. The birth of the internet, of course, disrupted the job search landscape with job-posting boards such as Monster.com cracking the market wide open at an unprecedented scale. Then, professional networking sites such as LinkedIn further changed the rules, enabling recruiters to find dormant job candidates. More recently, the new position of the HR Platform Sourcing Specialist—focused on using online platforms to find talent—indicates yet another shift.

As online talent platforms become mainstream, look to digital badging technology to be yet another bellwether of how the world of work will represent skills, education, and experiences in a more modular and portable way. Ask Wayne Skipper, founder of Concentric Sky, an award-winning software design and development firm. Wayne's evangelism of open technology standards gave rise to the microcredential platform Badgr, which has enabled companies, countries, and education systems to consider additional strategies for making candidates' skills, education, and experiences more transparent.

Badgr is an open-source digital badging infrastructure that has gained widespread adoption and is an innovation to watch. This digital method has the ability to provide the behind-the-scenes way for organizations to create stackable learning pathways and portable learner records. In a harbinger of broader adoption, Microsoft is now leveraging Badgr in the credentialing of skillsets and so is the Netherlands.

I happened to meet Wayne a few years ago when we both attended an Institute for the Future event and immediately fell into a conversation about technology developed for the common good (that is to say, the opposite of programs created to be proprietary to a company). We sat there amid the sprawling couches of IFTF's basement lounge, discussing the future workforce that our children will grow up into and the vital role digital badging most likely will play in that future.

"We just don't know what kinds of jobs today's toddlers will be applying for twenty years from now," Wayne mused. "But what we can predict is that by that time, AI will be much more sophisticated and powerful than it is today. Data science may actually be able to figure out what skills correlate with success in future jobs."

He helped me realize that neither he nor I had a crystal ball to show us the future of the shapeshifting importance of skills. After all, so many jobs are posted today that never existed a decade ago: Social Media Manager, Search Engine Optimization Specialist, App Developer, Driverless Car Engineer, Podcast Producer, Telemedicine Physician, and so on. As I pondered his insights, I gained a newfound appreciation for the concept of digital badges. Digital badges could be a powerful strategy for creating agility as the future of employment pivots.

Moving toward the Metrics of Mastery

Up until my conversation with Wayne, my exposure to digital badges had been limited to my son's online learning on Khan Academy, where mastering a certain unit of math earns students a badge. Sal Khan's brilliant approach to educating young people turned a system based on credit hours on its head. Rather than focusing on a fixed amount of time spent in a classroom between school bells, Khan only concerned himself with "time to mastery" as the metric, allowing students to excel and achieve at their own rates, earning badges as they went along. The 100 million young people growing up with this online competency-based model are learning with a level of agility that former generations wouldn't have been able to fathom at their age.

Even a few higher education institutions have broken from the credit hour paradigm to advanced competency-based learning. One of the first was Western Governors University. This fully accredited, online degree-granting institution also follows a learn-at-your-own-pace model, which allows students to graduate faster and pay less tuition. This approach provides a more inclusive way of looking at skills development and competencies appropriate for students who want to get a foot in the door despite otherwise not having the time or financial resources for a formal degree.

A degree can signal to a potential employer certain abilities that are proxies for skills, such as self-management and persistence. As mentioned in the prior chapter, Byron Auguste is a national advocate for giving opportunity to people who have acquired transferable skills but lack a formal degree. Using the acronym STARs (Skilled

Through Alternate Routes), Byron defines these as people at least twenty-five years of age who have transferable skills but not a higher education degree. To consider bypassing the use of formal degrees as a hiring screen means to shift emphasis onto skills and competencies. Digital badging could undoubtedly play a critical role in bridging the gap to conveying that person's skills and experiences to a potential employer.

In an article published by the Education Sector of New America over nine years ago, author Amy Laitinen challenged the notion of equating the credit hour to student learning. In a comprehensive twelve-hour exam that tested the "baccalaureate-level knowledge" of college freshmen, sophomores, juniors, and seniors, the results showed no correlation whatsoever between competency and credit hours. Since then, the conversation about finding new denominators of learning in higher education has grown more animated as surveys reveal an alarming disconnect between time spent in the classroom and job readiness. Less than 25% of employers believe graduates are prepared to start a career after college.

To prepare for the future of learning, colleges need what I call "air cover" to experiment. They must have some space for trial and error and familiarize themselves with new approaches until new processes became a part of their DNA. Then and only then will they be willing to embrace the risk.

Experimenting with Digital Badging
By the time I met Wayne Skipper, I'd been working as vice chancellor long enough to know that higher education institutions were

hesitant to adopt new strategies like digital badging, much less advocate for them. It would be my role in the state chancellor's office to invite experimentation.

In an earlier chapter, I spoke about the scarcity of twenty-first-century skills—otherwise known as soft skills—that employers so valued. A multi-college attempt to tackle these skills would make fertile grounds for our colleges to try out new strategies and gain experience with digital badging. First ten, then twenty, then sixty, and finally eighty-five community colleges adopted the resulting curriculum developed by Rajinder Gil and Amy Schulz, who also worked with Wayne to incorporate Badgr into experiments with digital badging. Students began to earn badges for demonstrating competencies along ten skills ranging from teamwork to entrepreneurial mindset. The education and social policy research organization MDRC observed the early positive student outcomes and proposed a longitudinal study on the curriculum, which was accepted by the US Department of Education Institute of Education Sciences.

Thanks to the experimentation, we went on to ask the next question: What else can be done with digital badging to aid students on their education journey? Sonya Christian, then president of Bakersfield College (and now chancellor of Kern Community College District) believed in guided pathways—a philosophy of simplifying how students navigated through the complex maze of college courses from entry to completion. Sonya, Wayne, and I huddled to brainstorm, and a program mapper became a twinkle of an idea.

A program mapper could present different learning pathways more clearly for students to reach a specific career goal. We created the

Pathways Program Mapper, a mobile-friendly website, first adopted by Bakersfield College, to lay out simple, semester-by-semester road maps of required courses from program entry to completion. Students exploring an associate degree for transfer could easily navigate up to nine meta-major pathways in subjects including health sciences, business administration, education, culinary arts, and accounting. Today, the Pathways Program Mapper, its design based on the digital badging system I introduced as an experiment, has already been adopted by thirty-three California community colleges and is on its way to being integrated into the California State University system. Researchers are looking at the on-path rate of students who use the tool, which has eliminated the differences of outcomes among ethnic groups, and are working to publish the positive findings.

By streamlining career education and also providing valuable data about related labor markets, California's community colleges are using the Pathways Program Mapper to help save students time and money by lowering the number of unnecessary classes they might take. Digital badging seems to have begun permeating the world of work and learning overnight.

Going Micro

In a world of unknowns, there are a few things that we as employers, educators, and government, labor, and community leaders do know about the current labor market: skills upgrades are key to workers who want to remain relevant in this type of ever-changing landscape. The agility that digital badging affords seems like a no-brainer when it comes to determining ways to mobilize competencies-based learning and potentially skills-based hiring.

In the race to keep up with the speed of need, and enabled by the digital badging infrastructure, microcredentials are poised to be a vital new strategy for curricular redesign and relevance. In a 2021 presentation entitled "Microcredentials: The Race Between Innovation and Public Regulation," Gillian Golden and Thomas Weko from the Organization of Economic Cooperation and Development (OECD) described how New Zealand, Australia, and Canada provided early examples of nondegree microcredentials appearing in public policy. They also shared the State University of New York (SUNY) academic guiding principles for shepherding the creation of microcredentials, signaling an evolution in higher education practices:

- Microcredentials designed to meet market needs should be informed by current data from appropriate markets and align with relevant industry/sector standards.
- Microcredentials can provide opportunities for industry/education connections and partnerships.
- Microcredentials are inherently more flexible and innovative.
- Microcredentials should be portable (have value beyond the institution).
- Microcredentials should be stackable (multiple microcredentials lead to credit-bearing coursework, a more advanced badge, or a registered certificate or degree).

From Dinosaur Thinking to Digital Native Innovation

In contrast to what I daresay will soon be called the "old days," detailed college transcripts may soon become a relic of the past. If you remember from chapter 4, Shalin Jyotishi described the experiments on interoperable learner record (ILR), a verifiable transcript of a person's achievements in education or training processes, whether classroom-based or on the job. As a nascent concept still undergoing experimentation, ILRs can be interchangeably shared among education providers and businesses, enabling portability of skills, education, and experiences. The agility of ILRs lies not only in their ability to identify when a learner's skills don't match those required by a hiring manager but also how learners might close this gap.

An article in *Educause* magazine brilliantly identifies the key components that make this type of agile data usage possible: "Understanding the data standards required by human resource information systems, as well as the definitional standards around skills, is essential in order to enable school-to-business, business-to-business, and business-to-school portability. Part of this challenge is linked to the need for open standards for data and skills taxonomies as part of a solution. Open standards allow for systems that read, compare, and share information inside a credential."

Credentials As You Go is a Lumina Foundation initiative that utilizes a nationally recognized incremental credentialing system to encourage the development of transferrable credentials beyond existing certificates and degrees. Holly Zanville, senior scholar and co-director of the program on skills, credentials, and workforce policy at George Washington University's Institute of Public Policy explained, "The traditional degree-centric system is punitive to many learners. It treats students who drop or stop out as if they have no college-level learning despite the growing array of shorter-term credentials they could earn which may be valuable to entering and advancing in the job market."

The trend toward agility is obvious. Let's take collaborative risks and familiarize ourselves with tools like digital badging and interoperable learner records to prepare for what is around the corner in the future of work. As I've said earlier, the digital natives already grew up with digital badging and skills-on-demand. Therefore, it's up to us to move away from dinosaur thinking and to reimagine higher education in the twenty-first-century landscape.

CHAPTER HIGHLIGHTS

- We need new social norms that call for continual upgrades in our education and skills throughout our lifetime, the way that software gets patched constantly. Digital natives will transition more readily than others.

- Digital badging, interoperable learner records, and microcredentials are strategies being employed by higher education and employers alike to wrestle with the shortened shelf life of skills and knowledge.

- Look to microcredentials as a new strategy for curricular redesign and relevance.

Nine

Harvesting Data for Improvement,
Freeing the Data

CHALLENGE:

How do we know we're moving the needle?

SOLUTION:

We must invest in data collection and
tools for calibrating supply and demand
and program outcome.

When I began my role as vice chancellor, in an effort to get to know the lay of the land, I would take trips into the rural Central Valley area to visit campuses within that region, rather than just tour those in the big metropolitan areas. At first, faculty and administrators seemed taken by surprise. The state chancellor's office had a reputation for staying near the state capital, and for anyone to make the three-hour drive (each way) just to understand their views was quite unexpected.

I also took many trips to the Inland Empire, a region that was often ignored because it stood in the shadow of Los Angeles. Every trip connected me with faculty, administrators, college partners, and students. Through the insights I gleaned, I began to detect common patterns, as well as learn to appreciate how regions differed. California is an amalgamation of regions. Just as states combine to create one nation while maintaining their individual characteristics, different regions within states have their shared interests but also different needs and wants.

Data—or to be more accurate, data deficiency—was a theme that I began to hear repeatedly. Workforce deans and college CEOs pointed to the system's metrics: Does the system have the right ones for our workforce mission? They asserted that the current metrics were appropriate for the system's transfer mission but did not recognize what students and employers valued when it came to workforce success. They posited that the lack of alignment was becalming their boat at a time when the economy needed wind in their sails. I took in every observation and recalled an adage of the business world: What is measured is what counts.

During the same period, I met Omid Pourzanjani, who was then the workforce dean at Golden West College. Like me, he was an immigrant and a former ESL student and had worked in industry prior to entering higher education. Omid came to the US at the age of fifteen accompanied only by his seventeen-year-old brother, because their parents got stuck during the Iranian revolution. His parents, like my own, wanted for them a better life and a good education. Omid and I discovered ourselves to be kindred spirits. Omid personally understood the challenges faced by students from underserved communities and made it his mission to promote equity, diversity, and inclusion in his higher education work.

When we met at a fateful community college conference in 2011, I noticed his formal manner of speech, possibly a residual of his upbringing in Iran, and he had kind eyes with an obvious high intellect behind every comment. We eventually became friends and allies, and he would later go on to bring his compassion and skills to his role as superintendent and president at San Joaquin Delta College, serving rural communities, after I left the California Community Colleges.

Our first encounter took place during a conference of all the community college workforce deans in the state only three months into my tenure. I delivered the expected state-of-the-state type of speech to the audience of 300 and proceeded to take questions from the floor. Omid stood up after a few others had spoken and said in a very no-nonsense tone, "Vice Chancellor, we need to free the data." Free the data. What did this odd statement mean? Which data? Was the state intentionally sitting on the voluminous archive of community college data? Omid's simple phrase, with its earnest delivery, had piqued my curiosity, to say the least.

I came to learn what Omid had in mind. Up until that point, our state systems office had required all 113 community colleges to load data into the system regularly that would ensure compliance with the legislature's various regulations. Metrics such as student attendance, enrollment numbers, and course completion all went toward the calculations that determined what revenues each college received. But this data-transfer relationship tended to go in only one direction. Harkening back to Al Gore's "lock box" analogy when he was running for US president, local data in a sense were being uploaded into the state repository, captured or "locked"—into a cycle of compliance reporting that offered little added value back to the colleges.

From the colleges' vantage point, they were doing a lot of work to give the chancellor's office their data and perceived the state to be sitting on a vault of valuable data—1 terabyte worth of it. The system had amassed data fully capable of providing intelligence to the colleges but only afforded by a bird's-eye view, just like my visits to all regions gave me novel insights into shared patterns and unique findings. I saw then, thanks to Omid's call to free the data, the potential to transition from just using data for the purpose of compliance reporting to creating tools that could enable our colleges to derive insights for decision-making and continuous improvement.

Measuring What Counts

As a reader, it's easy to zone out in a conversation on data, but experts know that it's really the secret sauce behind large system change. Often, new administrators and policy makers jump to the conclusion that funding is key—the more money, the better. Yes, but more funding is insufficient to beget the intended policy result. I have seen firsthand how sister public agencies, like the K–12 system, have gotten massive amounts of funds for new legislative programs to address workforce training, without much to show in the end. They had not sufficiently thought through the metrics and the data levers for how the funds would be used.

Monies, metrics, and data must align to beget big system change. The combined three can supercharge systemic change. I've developed this mantra after much experimentation and learning. And I will acknowledge up front that making changes to any one of these is hard enough—much less attempting to reshape all three. Without alignment, though, the best of policy-making intentions are undermined, often unknowingly.

Let me share an example for readers who care about student success and the transfer mission of community colleges. Omid would tell you that he answered the state's call for colleges to focus on student completion, not just the historical emphasis on creating broad access to higher education. He wanted to drive Golden West College to do the right things in order to graduate students efficiently and on time with the sixty credits needed to earn their associate's degree. The changes he implemented on campus across academic affairs and student services took root, and completion rates rose.

But his college financially ended up "getting punished" in the revenue formula. For you see, the state had a formula on how colleges would get paid—that is, colleges were paid based on how many students are enrolled in the third week of courses, otherwise known as "butts in seats." As an unintended consequence, his success in getting students to complete on time meant fewer students would be in the queue and hence his college received less revenue. What is measured is what counts.

Expunging Bad Data

Here's another key principle to remember: bad data in, bad data out. In cases where the data are used to inform high-stakes decisions on the back end—such as calculating how much revenue is awarded to each college—every institution is quite meticulous with its data entry. Notably, the state chancellor's office also implements auditing processes to catch errors. With the legislation putting in place the Strong Workforce Program, a new $200 million annualized funding stream that called for more and better career education programs, I had my work cut out for me to bring into alignment the monies, metrics, and data.

When it comes to workforce data, I heard across all the regions that the data collection process was cumbersome. For example, colleges received federal Carl D. Perkins Act money to support workforce programs in return for gainful employment reporting of students after graduation. Every community college took these grants. The allocation of these monies depended upon whether colleges were delivering on the promise of employability for students.

To collect the data, a subset of about sixteen colleges created a CTE Outcomes Survey and hired institutional researchers from Santa Rosa Community College to administer the process centrally.

Career education graduates would first receive an email, then a text, and, finally, a phone call to make sure they were answering questions such as, Were you able to get employment in the field that you studied? or What were you making two years before your studies and what type of wage gain did you experience six months and twelve months after graduation? These sixteen community colleges found a way to standardize the data collection method for their inventory of career education certificate and degree programs.

But what were the other ninety-seven colleges doing? I heard a common pattern while crisscrossing the regions. It turned out that faculty were spending an inordinate amount of time individually hunting for the data. How inefficient. I wondered, Why not expand this CTE Outcomes Survey to automate the data collection process, alleviating the burden across all the colleges and creating more reliable data feeds. With the freed time, faculty could better focus on the data's implications: How did students fare? Did they meet with workforce success as they desired and we intended?

Omid's call to free the data had gotten me to think about the role data played in higher education. Until this point, most college administrators were looking at data through the prism of compliance. Colleges did not want another accountability dashboard that rendered rewards and punishment by giving or taking revenues. I was curious to see what would happen if, instead, we used the data to propel us forward with insights, creating a tool to inform decision-making in keeping with ever-changing workforce needs.

I tasked my division at the chancellor's office to repurpose existing funds and invest in automating data feeds to ensure data quality and integrity. My division paid to extend the CTE Outcomes Survey to 100% of the colleges in the system. In addition, we increased in frequency, from once to four times a year, the data exchange our system already had in place with the Employment Development Division, which provided payroll data for our system, to ascertain whether students were working and what wages they earned. The data were anonymized to protect student privacy, but, because the feeds were consistent and automated from these reliable sources, they went a long way toward ensuring that the data that fed the system's data tools would be credible.

Data for Decision-Making

Making the data actionable was a surprising new concept taking seed at the time I started my tenure with the community colleges. Previously, data were mainly used only for compliance and account-ability. Knowing that any endeavor to launch a new data tool would require someone who understood the needs of campuses, I invited the one man I knew who would be up for the task.

"Omid, you asked me to free the data. If I do it, will you help by coming to the chancellor's office to lead the work?" I asked into the phone. "We need your expertise to make sure we do it right, and you speak the language of the field."

Upon becoming a visiting dean on my team and starting his weekly air commute from Southern California to Sacramento, Omid took charge of the political blocking and tackling of introducing concepts to a system that historically disliked data transparency. Until this point, data had been used to disclose shortcomings and deficits that would hinder colleges from receiving their funding.

Together with Kathy Booth of WestEd, a nonprofit organization providing complex program management, and Anthony Dalton of Education Results Partnership (ERP), a nonprofit specializing in higher education data science and data tool development, Omid went to work behind the scenes to help collectively design the first iteration of what eventually became the LaunchBoard.

With combined horsepower and ingenuity, Omid, Kathy, and Anthony (the trio of experts) conceived a data tool that would facilitate reflective and forward-thinking conversations among faculty and staff throughout California's community colleges, mobilize decision-making, and thereby free the data. Collectively, we understood that finding workforce outcome data was laborious for faculty and staff, who, by the time they got the results, were too tired to do anything about what the data told them. The trio believed that if the data sources could be automated to ensure integrity, then faculty and administrators would be free to focus on reflecting on the insights and taking action. The word *launch* in LaunchBoard, as Kathy explained, implied that the data would be used to catalyze additional conversations rather than be an end unto itself.

Making Data Agile

Version 1.0 of the LaunchBoard in 2014 was, to put it in technical terms, a flop. Designed only to answer a known set of questions, it failed to provide nuanced answers when questions were asked in a slightly modified way. For example, version 1.0 could give you the completion rate of a career education program; however, it could not show how completion rates fared across different student demographics or for the similar programs across different regions. So there we stood—Kathy, Omid, Anthony, and I—at the proverbial cliff. Faculty and administrators in the colleges were skeptical that the effort would yield anything of value. We took the risk, and LaunchBoard 1.0 wasn't a home run. We would be stuck unless we found a way to address stakeholders' desires and frustrations.

In the higher education world, if the data tool wasn't friendly or useful, we knew it would not "cross the chasm" into adoption. The phrase comes from Geoffrey Moore's influential book *Crossing the Chasm.* His technology adoption life cycle begins with innovators and moves to early adopters, early majority, late majority, and laggards—and acknowledges a vast chasm between the early adopters and the early majority. Higher education institutions were largely risk averse, and most preferred to sit things out and wait to see how their peers fared. LaunchBoard 1.0 was not ready for prime time.

As I have witnessed time and time again, the universe conspired to help crack this seemingly impossible situation by sending me Omid, Kathy, and Anthony, with their collective expertise. On their own, each was frustrated by their thwarted aspirations for the system's data, but here within an ecosystem of the willing, they could take the risks needed to get the job done.

Kathy's true gift was rooted in her understanding of the technical aspects of what needed to get done and being able to translate that understanding into layman's terms to bring along a diverse coalition of stakeholders to work together. To this end, Kathy convened over fifty people—workforce deans, institutional researchers, people in the systems office, and other longtime practitioners in the field—in a giant conference room to discuss the data problems they wanted to solve. With so many different players, it came as no surprise at the end of the session to see an entire wall covered in sticky notes marking the myriad needs and apprehensions of each group.

Kathy had decided to home in on the pressing questions asked by college career education faculty and deans so that LaunchBoard 2.0 would provide nuanced answers to address different levels of need. For instance, one campus vice president requested easy-to-read graphics with high-level, meaningful stats. In contrast, deans and institutional researchers at the meeting insisted on Excel spreadsheet-level granular data for them to analyze at a detailed level.

Anthony Dalton listened and rethought how LaunchBoard 2.0 could be redesigned to answer the range and variety of how the same question might be asked. Additionally, Anthony also saw how colleges and consortia of community colleges would download LaunchBoard data to create mini-dashboards, and he in turn integrated the most popular ones into the main tool.

Crossing the Chasm of Adoption

Taking everyone's concerns into account, the trio went back to the drawing board, deconstructing what had already been built, and inaugurated a version 2.0 of the LaunchBoard one year later, this time to widespread approval. I began hearing that campus practitioners who tried out LaunchBoard 2.0 in beta testing liked it and saw value in its use. I knew then that the tool was good. That shifted us into the rollout phase. If colleges were willing to test it, they were certain to see its agility and usefulness. Like in that old Life cereal commercial from the 1970s, I thought, all I have to do is get Mikey to try it, and he'll like it! What we needed now was a plan to go to scale and incentivize all 113 campuses to use the tool.

We had to overcome known objections if we were to successfully gain adoption by 100% of the colleges in the largest system of higher education in the country. These were the most common ones: We don't have the resources to clean up our data. We can't proceed if this tool is not incorporated into our accreditation reporting. We need our faculty trained to use the tool.

To address these three objections, we gave colleges across the board a very attractive offer. We guaranteed each college a $50,000 grant if they agreed to send a campus team to attend LaunchBoard training. And all teams had to include an executive leader. Why? To make sure that every campus had an executive champion who understood the tool and could speak from a position of confidence were they to need to defend the information that came out of it.

The $50,000, once unlocked, could be used (1) to clean up their data input to ensure quality output, thus putting to rest the complaint of bad data, (2) to undertake the technical integration with their accreditation reporting system, or (3) to make sure that faculty could get the proper training to use the LaunchBoard. Looking ahead to where colleges could stumble when using the tool, the trio also appointed a group of superusers who received a stipend to learn the tool with sufficient depth and paired every college with them to pass that training on.

Making Data Actionable and Equitable

Almost immediately, some opposed the use of the LaunchBoard because they believed it operated based on bad data. Because of the concerted effort up front to ensure data integrity, we knew to point out that the data reflected what they had entered, and if they thought it wrong, they needed to clean up what they input. The $50,000 onetime grant provided the funds to perform that task.

Among colleges who trusted the data, some did not like what they saw. Anecdotal evidence and uneven data sources had fed perceptions of their students' success up to this point. The LaunchBoard displayed findings that were usually consistent but sometimes contradictory. For example, in San Diego a small group of faculty got together to discuss their LaunchBoard data and, seeing that enrollment and completion rates were high, congratulated themselves on a job well done. However, once they trained their eyes on the data for workforce outcome, they saw that very few graduates had actually secured employment. They realized that, even with high enrollment and completion, they could be missing the mark in terms of workforce outcome.

Before the advent of LaunchBoard, this was where the conversation would have ended. No longer burdened with having to hunt for the data, this faculty group did exactly what we had intended with the tool—they discussed lack of student success and created a plan on what needed to happen next.

Linking Data to the Labor Market

Access to the LaunchBoard gave faculty members insights into the labor market to help them keep their career education programs from getting stale. As we have seen throughout this book, unlike the slower cadence of general education where faculty can afford to ruminate before making changes to course material, the adaptation of employment-geared curricula must take place at the rapid speed of changing business cycles. Even among the eighty-three in-demand nursing programs offered through California's community colleges, while some were exemplars when it came to completion rates, others needed some continuous improvement.

Within the LaunchBoard, using a lookup function, faculty from colleges were able to contact their peers at others to glean advice. This kind of built-in social reinforcement fostered a sense of community practice that started to replace the competitiveness that had formerly alienated colleges. In fact, faculty were eager to discover how comparable colleges under the same array of regulatory and financial constraints within California fared. Then, by speaking with other instructors and learning about their better practices, they could start to make decisions about where to invest their own resources. For example, if the only factor differentiating a better-performing college from its peers was hiring a dedicated student success coordinator, then other colleges might choose to allocate part of their budgets to adopt a similar staffing strategy.

With the idea of actionable data in mind, we automated EMSI, a labor market analytics firm, to feed us their labor market and wage data in order for colleges to view employment and employability beyond their local context. Since roughly 80% of community college students stayed within their region after graduation, it was important to find out whether programs were over-supplying or under-supplying the regional labor market. Again, the data would offer insights on whether colleges should continue these programs or begin to shift investments into other opportunities. By automating the data, colleges no longer needed to spend valuable time hunting for it themselves.

Braiding Funds into Something Meaningful

You might wonder how we found the funds to develop such a tool. Let me explain the tried-and-true magic of braiding. Braiding, unlike integrating funds, continues to honor rather than ignore the requirements of the funding stream. Debra Jones, my lieutenant in the chancellor's office, started by repurposing small pots, sometimes as little as $1,000, and eventually braiding in more as we freed up monies elsewhere and secured new resources. We grew from $100 million in responsibility to over $1 billion over my eight-year tenure. Every program in the $1 billion portfolio had a data and reporting requirement. Instead of approaching the requirement in silo, why not braid funds across all the programs to build the unified data tool and use it to serve all three programs?

Every public funding stream has strings attached, and we had to be careful not to sever those strings. Not surprisingly, each program always had an associated data collection and reporting requirement. Once we realized that the reporting requirements of all the workforce programs were all similar in nature—including the Carl A. Perkins Act, the Economic and Workforce Development, the Apprenticeship Innovation Program, the Adult Education Block Grant, and the Strong Workforce Program—we knew we could braid the dollars from each to create a tool that not only delivered that rearview mirror compliance reporting but also what colleges wanted, which was a data tool to inform decision-making and continuous improvement.

Unintended Positives

In the end, we chipped away at all known objections to adopting a new data tool. Furthermore, we tightly linked the use of the tool to how the new $200-million-a-year Strong Workforce Program monies would flow in 2016, creating a big incentive for colleges to get on board. By the time I left office, the LaunchBoard had become the data system undergirding the whole system. In fact, a few years after its initial rollout, a new system chancellor came aboard with an agenda to implement guided pathways as his signature program, aiming to help students complete their education objectives in a more focused and efficient way. Twenty community colleges participated in the first-round technical assistance community of practice.

When it came to adopting a data system, the group of twenty was faced with three choices during their summer meeting in 2017: import a system developed in New York, which would take up to a year's time; create something from scratch, which would take at least two years; or use the LaunchBoard, for which staff had already been trained, and which would take two months. Of course, the best choice was at this point a no-brainer. At the two-month mark, the LaunchBoard went live with a tab for the new program and functionally became the data tool not only for the workforce but also for the transfer missions of the California Community Colleges. That is a higher education exemplar in being agile.

In the final chapter of this book, I will look at a part of our economy that demands agile responses. Let's look at ways to advance the gig economy, how it demands a relook at our human infrastructure, and whether we have yet to set up what it takes for workers and the workforce to thrive.

CHAPTER HIGHLIGHTS

- When it comes to how institutions behave, it's what is measured that counts.
- Deficiency of data is a ubiquitous problem, leading to ill-informed or even uninformed decisions.
- Wrong metrics can undermine policy intentions.
- Use of funds should be informed with accurate and objective data. "The more money the better" isn't good enough.
- For real effective change in public policy, the money, metrics, and data have to align.
- Harvesting data for continuous improvement is essential.
- Using bad data input will erode trust in the tools.
- Designing data to be actionable leads to better decisions, since the point in collecting information is to then catalyze action.

Ten

Getting Ahead of the Gig

CHALLENGE:

How do we build the right infrastructure
to help gig workers thrive?

SOLUTION:

We must re-conceptualize employer
assets to make them portable and transferrable.

The Future of Assets

When I stepped down after two terms with the California Community Colleges, as an appointee under Governor Jerry Brown serving as vice chancellor and then executive vice chancellor, I was completely exhausted from driving higher education reform—doing what one dean called "teaching dinosaurs to dance." As you may remember from prior chapters, I recounted stories of how easy it is to become personally regarded as a dinosaur these days given the rapid evolution of technology. Perhaps the better analogy would be chasing tortoises and hares; with so many institutions involved, their agility would be predictably uneven. I needed to renew myself and get the bounce back into my step and took a sabbatical as executive-in-residence at the Institute for the Future (IFTF).

As the name suggests, the mission of this global organization, housed right in the heart of Silicon Valley, is to provide foresight into what the world will look like in the ten-year horizon—tracing signals of the future from current events—in food, health, self, transportation, commerce, city planning, and more. IFTF creates what it refers to as actionable insights on the cutting edge of economics, technology, and trade that are helpful to leaders of organizations across the globe.

In 2019, when multiple governors formed future of work task forces, IFTF was retained to shape California's effort by Governor Gavin Newsom's administration. The Institute's staff had been focusing for years on the future of work in its body of research as more and more seismic shifts created waves in the world of work.

Among these shifts is the movement toward the relatively new concept of worker co-ops as professionals begin to lose the security of permanent employment. Playing a similar role to that of a trade union, such co-ops afford gig workers and independent contractors, at minimum, the buying power for assets like health insurance and retirement plans. Must choosing flexibility always means forfeiting the healthcare benefits and retirement plans typically tied to regular full-time employment arrangements?

While worker co-op structures are commonplace outside of the US and tend to be prevalent within the agricultural industry and credit unions domestically, until now, they have been rare among white-collar workers in this country. In a timely article written for *Quartz*, Marina Gorbis, observes the fact that as a nation we are creating jobs with few, if any, assets.

> Open a newspaper—or, more likely, click on a Facebook article on your phone—and there will be a story telling you that income inequality is at the root of America's problems: 0.1% of the US population is worth almost as much as the bottom 90%; CEO-to-worker pay ratios have increased a thousandfold since 1950; and wages have been stagnating for 35 years . . . But while the wages we are paid are vital to the success and comfort of our lives, economic returns have been going increasingly to investors rather than wage earners. The real affliction America is suffering from isn't income inequality: It's asset inequality.

Since we can't put the genie back in the bottle, so to speak, the question becomes, How do we restore these assets to protect the worker of the future? In a McKinsey article based on a poll of 800 executives across various industries, generally positive predictions about the future of work are still tinged with this concern:

> Greater digitization and automation, more demand for independent contractors, and increased reliance on remote work have the potential to deliver better productivity, lower costs, and enhance resilience . . . The trick will be in reducing the risk of unequal outcomes, ensuring companies of all sizes can benefit, and preparing workers for these shifts.

Worker co-ops have been established in other countries for decades, proving their popularity and sustainability. In the Basque region of Spain sits the world's largest industrial co-op with 85,000 worker-owners and annual sales of $20 billion. In the northern Italy region, 4.5 million people are worker-owners within Emilia Romagna, a networked ecosystem of co-ops across many industries, which produces one-third of the region's GDP. Clearly, the model can operate at scale.

The co-op model has also proved to be an interesting experiment in the US. Take a look at the Cooperative Home Care Associates (CHCA) created in New York in 1986. CHCA provides home health services and employs 2,500 worker-owners who have notably very low employee turnover as compared to the industry; 65% of new

CHCA hires remained in their jobs at the one-year mark compared to 37% in comparable organizations, according to a 2016 Workforce Benchmarking Network Survey. Some 80% of CHCA's revenues go to worker wages and benefits.

CoRise Cooperative is a family childcare co-op in Illinois created to employ the state's 35,000 childcare workers. Arizmendi Association of Cooperatives is a co-op network in California operating a federation of six bakeries, landscaping design/build, and housing constructions co-ops. AlliedUP, launched in 2021 as a new venture, is a worker co-op placement agency for allied health workers.

Worker co-ops have the potential for scale and represent a frontier for experimentation on how to create jobs with assets. This matters because credential attainment alone cannot lead to an inclusive economy when the nature of work is undergoing redefinition.

The pandemic's unequal impact on minority communities, compounded by the Black Lives Matter movement, brought attention to unequal economic outcomes in the country. Even before then, worker advocacy groups and labor unions united on the issue, and the convergence led to Assembly Bill 5, passed in California in September 2019, which reclassified gig workers to offer them worker protections such as overtime pay and paid leave, which were unavailable to those whose livelihoods were based on online platforms. Assembly Bill 5 effectively codified standards for determining which workers would be classified as independent contractors instead of employee status, a ruling with big financial implications.

The legislation was targeted particularly at rideshare (for example, Uber and Lyft) and food delivery services (such as Instacart,

DoorDash, and Postmates). Research from Barclays estimated that Uber had approximately 140,000 drivers in California in 2019 and Lyft had 80,000. Unsurprisingly, given the companies' size in the state, the CEOs of both Uber and Lyft came out in opposition and waged an expensive war to oppose the legislation. Uber and Lyft, along with a few other platform companies, applied $205 million to sponsor a ballot measure, Proposition 22, the following year which ended up passing. Proposition 22 created a loophole that exempted platform companies from being subject to Assembly Bill 5. Big money was at stake in defining the shifting landscape of the future of work.

As a bellwether, a landmark event occurred in March 2021 in Europe, mirroring the debates that waged around Assembly Bill 5. The 70,000 Uber drivers in Britain were reclassified as employees, thus making them eligible for minimum wage, vacation pay, and access to a pension plan. Admittedly, this verdict by the British Supreme Court came about only after years of litigation and strife between Uber and the company's gig workers.

These big public struggles aside, my hope and belief is that the future of assets can evolve more organically, and this frontier is ripe for experimentation. What are the models for workers to gain access to assets like healthcare and retirement plans, knowing that more work and workers will go the way of online platforms? As someone whose focus has been on the skilling and upskilling of workers, I can see around the corner that workers will need new human infrastructures than what exists today. We need new playbooks and now is the time to seed experimentation with viable models.

Capitalism with Heart

While I was at the Institute for the Future, Marina introduced me to Howard Brodsky who, for thirty-three years, has been at the helm of CCA Global Partners, one of the largest retail conglomerates in America, serving over one million family businesses. Howard is a generous and thoughtful person whose white hair and bearing remind me a bit of the actor Christopher Plummer from *The Sound of Music*. I recently had the pleasure of interviewing Howard on my Workforce Rx podcast to discuss the ins and outs of worker co-ops.

According to Howard, a shared ownership model inherent in worker co-ops is the key to boosting employee retention dramatically while increasing their wealth at the same time. He shares evidence on why this model is compelling for this moment in time as our nation wrestles with whether we have adequate human infrastructures pairable with the gig economy of the future of work.

With an estimated 25 to 30% of family businesses failing in the US during the COVID pandemic, the closure rate among CCA Global's members, who are all co-ops, has only been a comparatively minuscule 1 to 2%. I quickly learned from Howard that the strength of the co-op model lies in the concept of ownership. Not only are members invested in the decision-making, but they also share in the financial profits that would normally go to shareholders.

"There are two types of poverty that we have in the world and in the United States," said Howard. "I think there's poverty of economics and there's poverty of hope. What co-ops do is they address both of those issues . . . They [also] give you scale without losing control and give you the tools you need to compete against any large company in the world." These ideas are behind what Howard calls capitalism with heart, and they represent a possible playbook for these unsettled times.

On the same podcast episode, Howard and I discussed at length the possibilities of applying the co-op model to home care workers, who are notoriously underpaid. In the current hiring model, if a patient needs a home attendant, they pay an agency $25 to $35 an hour, of which the agency in turn distributes only $12 to $14 to the attendant. Howard calls this dynamic a component of the "extraction economy" in which a disproportionate amount of the money goes to the collector compared to the person doing the actual work.

What if the co-op model could be applied to the over four and a half million employed home care workers? Not only would the retention rate of these workers increase, but the chances of attracting enough new workers to fill the current shortage of a million and a half would go up incredibly. By forming a co-op, workers could earn $22 an hour, nearly doubling their wages. Perhaps just as important is the possibility of providing workers with benefits, such as access to their own healthcare at a cheaper cost.

In addition, discounts on gas cards and car insurance would allow them to take home even more money. To take this projected model a step further, since the home care worker is the one who knows exactly which medical supplies are needed for each patient in the home, part of the co-op's responsibility could be to provide these supplies at no extra cost to the patient but with a slight profit going toward the home care attendant, thus bringing up their income even more.

Paying It Forward through Community-Subsidized Training

While it's exciting to discuss theoretical problem solving with innovative thinkers like Howard, I believe it's only a matter of time before whole industries will be able to implement these strategies to revolutionize worker compensation as well as upskilling. And I am not alone in this line of thinking. Serving as an executive-in-residence opened my mind in thinking that perhaps our current social structures and public infrastructure are insufficient for the next economy.

Six months after I stepped down from my California Community Colleges position mid-2019, Dave Regan, president of SEIU–UHW, a union of nearly 97,000 hospital healthcare workers, came to me with a novel concept his team had been working on for two years. With the structure of the labor union in decline, Dave had been observing the new ways workers were organizing themselves to give voice to their needs. He was particularly intrigued by how co-op structures influenced scale, worker mobility, and worker assets. More so because healthcare was highly credentialed as a condition of employment, Dave wondered whether there was a way workers in his union could fund the education needed to grow the next generation of healthcare workers, giving opportunity to those who could not access it on their own.

To pay for the education, Dave's idea was a scaled version of paying it forward, so to speak, financed through a form of tithing into which the members would contribute. Matched by employer contributions, the resulting funds would enable friends and family of his union member to affordably earn a healthcare credential.

Students, at the end of the education journey, would be invited to become a worker-owner in a new co-op staffing agency that specialized in allied health postings. The co-op would serve as the employer-of-record to graduates, finding them work and also providing them with stable healthcare and retirement benefits regardless of how many clients or how long they worked with any client on an assignment. As worker-owners of the co-op, they would share in any profits made by the organization.

This innovative vision of community-subsidization would alleviate the reliance on traditional public sources of student loans as well as alleviate the burden on the individual who may not have the means to earn their own credentials and move up the ladder.

His articulated concepts were bold, and I saw within the ideas another possible playbook for dealing with the missing human infrastructures needed for workers to thrive in future work. I was intrigued. With help from Tammy Johns, a petite, smart-talking Canadian and former Manpower executive, I went to work molding Dave's bold ideas in reality and laid the groundwork for the 2020 launch of Futuro Health, of which I'm chief executive officer.

A year later, AlliedUP, the worker co-op part of the concept came into being with seasoned staffing executive Carey Carpineta at its helm. Combined, the two organizations—one nonprofit and the other a worker co-op (by definition, co-ops are for-profit legal structures)—serve as a living lab to refine the innovation playbook that could enable increased worker resilience as the future of work shifts further into the gig economy.

Building an Ecosystem of Trust

I must admit, I had little understanding of unions initially. My first exposure to one came in my thirties while at PG&E creating the PowerPathway workforce development program. In my role heading up workforce development, I was introduced to the company's apprenticeship program, jointly run by the company and its union, the International Brotherhood of Electrical Workers (IBEW) Local 1245. I used my listening skills to study how this union functioned.

For instance, IBEW representatives Landis Marttila and Hunter Stern made it clear that while they must protect workers' interests once hired, they would be open-minded and willing to support my efforts to source quality diverse candidates pre-hire. They, too, favored the company making good hires and wanted to avoid addressing performance-quality issues down the road. Admittedly, not all unions and their leaders share IBEW's philosophy, but IBEW signaled an interest in joining the ecosystem of the willing.

I spent five years working with Landis and Hunter, engaging in continuous problem solving while I was with PG&E. IBEW even endorsed my participation in panels hosted by the AFL-CIO and their umbrella organization, the California Labor Federation, to speak on the playbook we employed to diversify and fortify the frontline workforce for PG&E, whom IBEW represented and who were at risk of aging out. This workforce included utility workers, line workers, system operators, and welders. The story was a win-win-win for the employer, union, and community.

Years later, as vice chancellor, I gleaned another valuable lesson about the nature of unions, namely that they can be very slow to trust. Three months into my position, I noticed on my calendar that a meeting had been scheduled with a union that I had never met, SEIU–UHW, which in the world of state politics stands above others for their savvy. New to the state capital, I had no background on the political force that took up seats in the room, so when I stepped inside, I did what I normally do and asked, How can I help you?

The seconds of silence that followed told me this was not the way meetings with SEIU–UHW typically were started. Then, Rebecca Miller, their vice president who had brought the twenty people to the meeting, explained that they were not used to such an open welcome. In fact, she explained, SEIU–UHW members were usually met with some wariness. It turns out, Rebecca had convened the meeting for a very specific reason. She needed help from the community colleges to skill up SEIU–UHW's members and wanted to tap into affordable ways for them to earn additional healthcare credentials. SEIU–UHW even had monies to pay and did not need to tap into public funds. They were troubled by the localized higher education system that was too vast and complicated for them to navigate, even with funds to spend. That day, we inaugurated a long-standing working relationship that grew as the union observed me in action, sometimes from afar and other times up close.

One of the issues on which we strongly came together was the need to streamline curriculum approval. The slow speed of this process was an impediment to the timely turnaround of relevant career education programs that could make students more employable. I remember sharing this concern in a conference of a dozen community college chancellors and presidents in Los

Angeles. When I spoke of the need to streamline the curriculum process, one venerable leader lamented that he had been in the system for twenty-five years and, for that entirety, the same issue had plagued the community colleges. The nut would be tough to crack, he implied.

Joining me for a series of conversations with the faculty senate, a union-like structure of community college instructors, SEIU–UHW demonstrated a surprising willingness to put itself on the line for some rather controversial conversations—even putting them at odds with their labor peers. Over the course of seven and a half years, our relationship grew as we operated in a trusted ecosystem of the willing. Thanks to Rebecca Miller's support as a strong ally and her spitfire determination to navigate complicated political waters, legislation passed that mandated the streamlining of the curriculum-approval process. No one of us could have done this feat on our own.

SEIU–UHW was not alone in the ecosystem of the willing. The California Chamber of Commerce, California Manufacturing and Technology Association, California Hospital Association, California EDGE Coalition, ACLU, and others joined me in expressing support to pass the Strong Workforce Program legislation.

Of note, James Mayer, CEO of California Forward, an organization that paid attention to the triple bottom line issues affecting equity, environment, and economics, combined forces with SEIU–UHW to go door-to-door to ask the governor and leaders of the legislature to pass the bill that I had helped conceive.

The Strong Workforce Program was signed into law in 2016 and expanded community college career education programs to the tune of $200 million per year. Never before had workforce programs received that significant an injection of resources, especially on an ongoing basis.

I already knew, but once again appreciated, that I could solve seemingly intractable, long-standing problems through collaboration. For big structural issues, no one institution or organization can find the solution. I made more progress through collective action than I could have on my own. This is the power of the ecosystem of the willing.

Designing for Scale

I have always loved to design, approaching it with the same curiosity and playfulness with which many people dig into a good crossword puzzle. I seem to have a gift for understanding big systems and organizations and how to factor in the needed changes. While some people like to maintain what is already established, I thrive when I have to come up with new solutions and grow something. That's why I started listening very closely when Dave Regan asked me to help build Futuro Health from the ground up.

"Van," he said, upon explaining his concept of training the next generation of healthcare workers and employing them in a co-op, "what would it take for you to be CEO and help us make this concept that we have into a reality?"

It didn't take long for me to agree to put on my hard hat, roll up my sleeves, and dig in. There was just one thing: I told Dave that he needed to deliver on the capital to do the work, and I would focus on the execution. On those terms, I was on board.

Dave told me I had a two-year ramp. Once I got started, several voices of self-doubt resounded throughout my mind. If I looked in the rearview mirror, I was fully aware of my previous accomplishments. I'd already taken a very complex, massive, public higher education system from $100 million to over $1 billion during an eight-year period. I was tempted to rest on my laurels, knowing that if I strived for something new that had never been done before, success was far from guaranteed. I risked failure at this late stage of my career. The pestering voice of judgment I spoke about in a previous chapter was once more telling me to stop while I was ahead.

Instead of listening to that voice, however, I decided to plow forward. I started the work part-time in August 2019 and then was engaged full-time a month later.

The same fall, SEIU–UHW and the major multi-state healthcare system Kaiser Permanente found themselves in the throes of a wicked collective bargaining fight. If an agreement could not be reached, a strike would occur, which meant 56,000 of Kaiser Permanente's employees would stop work across hospitals and care facilities. The tension was high. At 4:00 a.m. on the last day of negotiations that mid-October night, a compromise was reached.

Both parties committed to set aside $130 million within the collective bargaining agreement to train the next generation of healthcare workers. Because I had been doing the legwork with Dave Regan, the creation of Futuro Health was top of mind as he weathered the final moments of the negotiations. The next morning, Dave announced that the first payment of $32.5 million in the nonprofit would be transferred on January 1. My two-year on-ramp shrank to a measly two and a half months. Moving at the speed of need, I launched Futuro Health by the deadline.

The board members of Futuro Health met for the first time to formally establish its charter in December 2019. On January 1, $32.5 million was transferred. Eight days into 2020, we launched Futuro Health to the public. Within a year's time, Futuro Health enrolled 1,691 adult students into a variety of quality higher education programs that would enable adults from all walks of life to earn their industry-valued credential.

The pandemic has shown that the speed of need slows for no one. Now is the time to experiment and be ready for possible futures by trying out bold ideas involving scale, collaboration, ecosystems, private-public infrastructures, community subsidies, co-ops, and capitalism with a heart. Once we collectively understand playbooks that work, let's not suffer from thinking too small with no road map for scaling success—or pilot fatigue as I called it in chapter 5.

Instead, if we design experiments with the intention to scale, we can use advance public policies to reinforce and replicate good practices, spreading them through networked institutions backed by smart metrics and data tools. These unsettled moments are the time to uncover what works even as our voices of judgment suggest that the status quo is just fine. As James Mayer, 2021 National Public Service Award winner and longtime ally, neighbor, olive farmer, and policy expert, would say to me, "If not us, then who will take on these hard issues?"

Immigrants into the Future

We are all immigrants into the future. I first heard that phrase at the Institute for the Future. I loved it so much that I ended my commencement keynote with this phrase. I delivered a future of work talk at the graduation ceremony of Golden Gate University students who earned masters and doctoral degrees in business, taxation, and accounting. These adult students fretted over whether AI would take over their jobs and requested a speaker who could speak on the future of work, hoping to glean an antidote.

None of us can predict the future, including me, but I know of ways we can still prepare. Specific to the workforce, I know for certain that the future will demand a more agile set of practices and human infrastructure to weather future changes and support workers and employers.

Over the past fourteen years, I have solved talent shortages for companies, shepherded private-public partnerships in order to yield quality inclusive talent pools, reshaped the practices and tools of community colleges and government to get more people in our communities into good jobs and to value workforce as a public-policy priority, and advised national discourse on the interplay between higher education and the economy. In every chapter of this book, I hope readers have benefited from highlights of real case studies and personal anecdotes to illustrate the guiding principles of agility.

With an eye toward the burgeoning gig economy, I hope you have found within this book some practical approaches to the challenges facing work, workers, inclusion, and the economy today. My even greater hope is that employers and educators, and government, labor, and community leaders will continue to approach workforce development with an agile mindset and a collaborative spirit to ready us to move ahead of the speed of need.

Paying Opportunity Forward

Let me end with one final personal story. As you may recall from the beginning of this book, I have always cared about education and creating the same kinds of opportunities for others that were given to me when I came to the US as an immigrant from the Vietnam War. I was selected into an executive development program for mid-career professionals, called the Leadership Fellows Program of the International Women's Forum (IWF). The IWF is an invitation-only global membership organization of women who represent the top females in their organizations and field. This group hosted the fellows program to develop the next generation of women leaders. While the majority of the fellows in my 2000–2001 cohort were US based, our group had representation from Australia, Canada, and South Africa as well. I was in my early thirties, while others were mostly in their forties.

These women have since gone on to achieve a range of success, from selling their thriving companies, to providing leadership over major state and federal agencies, to heading up enterprises and global operations for brand-name corporations. Our group gathered annually to exchange updates and seek one another's advice on personal and career challenges. We had to navigate layoffs, corporate restructuring, family and health issues, personal insecurities, and more.

In this trusting environment, these women gave me powerful feedback on a behavior that I appeared to repeat from job to job—and that impeded my success. The substance of the matter had to do with how I dealt with a type of uncomfortable situation: when the boss and I differed in our opinion on what to do, I would shut down instead of exploring an alternative approach. As hard to hear as the advice was, I took the feedback to heart and found a personal coach to help me create different ways to react should a similar situation arise. It worked. My career skyrocketed after that, and so did my impact and reach when it came to being able to pay forward opportunity to others.

As we navigate the future of work that we want, we should heed the feedback that may not be easy to hear. How does higher education retain its relevance? Do corporations have accountability for inclusive practices? Do education and training suffice if the work people do offers no assets?

If our human infrastructure needs to be reshaped because we want a future in which people and communities inclusively thrive, acting on these signals will not be easy. As I've pointed out in chapter 2, it will be a team sport. I hope this book has equipped you with more playbooks than you owned before by unlocking solutions you may not have otherwise considered as strategies. I wish you the best and hope you can help me continue to unlock opportunity for others.

CHAPTER HIGHLIGHTS

- The future of work demands new playbooks that deliver on agility, always with inclusion in mind.

- Getting ahead of the gig, the human and social infrastructures needed for work and workers to be resilient in an increasingly gig economy can be a stabilizing force to households.

- Look to worker owned co-ops and community-subsidized training as scalable models for resolving some of the pitfalls in the future of work.

- Unsettled times serve as good moments for experiments that, if proven successful, can be taken to scale and be reinforced by public policies.

- We are all immigrants into the future. What we can do now is prepare and decide on the future we want.

Acknowledgments

In addition to the individuals who were mentioned in these chapters, I would like to express my appreciation to all of you who have cheered me on:

Gayatri Agnew

Amrit Ahluwalia

Nina & Alex Antebbi

Hortencia Armendariz

Veenu Aulakh

Manuel Baca

Barbara Baran

Geoffrey Baum

Mary-Ann Bell

Amanda Bergson-Shilcock

Helen Benjamin

Chokri BenSaid

Mike Bernick

Joseph Bielanski

Keith Bird

Marlene Blasco

Siobhan Brady

Jeremy Koch

John Brauer

Cheryl Broom

Denise Brosseau

Jack Buckhorn

Chris & Lisa Buehler

Earl Buford

Ryan Burke

Daniel Bustillo

Walter Bumphus

Brian Burrell

Lindsey Brie

Peter Callstrom

Sam Campana

David Carlisle

Michael Carrese

Stephanie Carrillo

Constance Carroll

Judy Catambay

Alan Chan

Scott Cheney

John Chiang

Darren Chidsey

Frank Chong

Suzie Chun

Ed Coghlan

Tom Cohenno

Sam Collazo

Beth Cobert

Sam Combs

Tyson Conn

Shawn Cooper

John Cordova

Geoffrey Cox

Ryan Craig

Ra Criscitiello

Sun & Mark Culpepper

Tim Cuneo

Brenda Curiel

Imelda Dacones

Gina Dalma

Brenda Dann-Messier

Ashwini Davison

Tom Dawson

Kari Decker

Brooke DeRenzis

Emily Stover DeRocco

Beth Devin

Nataly Diaz

Gora Dotta

Mike Dozier

Eric Drummond

William Duncan

John Dunn

Jennifer Edson

Cindy Eisenberg

Karen Elzey

Tom Epstein

Tom Ehrlich

Camille Esch

Nick Esquivel

Cecilia Estolano

Chad Evans

Jaime Fall

Paul Fain

Helen Fairchild

Jennifer Lee Farrell

Chris Ferguson

David Fike

Chris Flask

Kevin Fleming

Brenda Fong

Jeffrey Forrest

Paul Fong

Wyman Fong

Jessica Fraser

Larry Galizio

Jane Garcia

Marlene Garcia

Rob Garcia

Elaine Gaertner

Alex Gil

Carole Goldsmith

Larry Good

Grant Goold

Wendy Gordon

Claire Grady

Walter Greenleaf

David Grossman

Cass Gualvez

Nancy Gutierrez

Oscar Gutierrez

Jean Hagan

Sandy Hagerty

Amy & Borge Hald

John & Carol Hamilton

Virginia Hamilton

Ammar & Faiza Hanafi

Bryan Hancock

Rebecca Hanson

Anne Happel & Toby Wehrhan

Brice Harris

Bruce Harland

Flannery Hauck

Pamela Haynes

Carla Hebert-Kirby

Judy Heiman

Joy Hermsen

Monica Henestroza

Gustavo Herrera

Brian Hertzog

Lily Hickman

Heidi Hill Drum

Matt Horton

Doug Houston

Victor Hu

Laura Huober

Glenda Humiston

John Husing

Sue Hussey

Vicky Jackson

Louise Jaffe

Parminder Jassal

Suzanne Jiminez

Joyce Johnson

Sally Johnstone

Craig Justice

Kermit Kabela

Tom Kalinske

Mike Kanazawa

Martha Kanter

Amy Kaufman

Kuldeep Kaur

Trish Kelly

Shelley Kessler

Brian King

Mary Kimball

Mike Kirst

Stewart Knox

Ed Knudsen

Aarti Kohli

Bernie Kotlier

Uta Kremer

Stewart Knox

Ed Knudson

Juliana Kumpf

George & Signe Kurian

Martha Laboissiere

John Ladd

Mary Beth Lakin

Bob Lanter

Phuoc & Nhien Le

Anita Lee

Rayna Lehman

Jill Leufgren

Liza Leyva

Janet Liang

Michelle Look

Tracey Lovejoy

Susan Lovenburg

Suzanne Louie

Stewart Louis

Shannon Lucas

Stan Lyles

Melinda Mack

Amber Mace

Jeff Maggioncalda

Jannet Malig

Debbie Malumed

Rishi Manchanda

Gabe Manjarrez

Kathy Mannes

Cathy Martin

Mark Martin

Joe May

Laurie McGraw

Brian McKeown

Brian McMahon

Ned McCulloch

Bill McGinnis

Patrick McNellis

Ken McNeill & Julie Pelletier

John Means

Gustavo Medina

Girard Melancon

John Melville

Totsie Memela Khambula

Lenny Mendonca

Steve Mendoza

Satish Menon

Linda Michalowski

Jose Millan

Marilyn Millington

Cindy Miles

David Miller

Keetha Mills

Kevin Mills

Judy Miner

Leah Moehle Grassini

Marie Mookini

Steve & Charlene Morales

James Morante

Becky Morgan

Roxana Moussavian

Kathy Moxon

Jeffrey Mrizek

Kevin Mullin

Sunita Mutha

Ricardo Navarrette

Heath Nash

Katie Nielson

Michele Nguyen

Thuy Nguyen

Jonathan Njus

Eloy Oakley

Jane Oates

John Oehmke

Stephanie O'Keefe

Rory O'Sullivan

Anne Palmer

Janet Payne

Roslyn Payne

Scott Paul

Carole Pepper-Kittredge

Patrick Perry

Carrie Portis

Ram Prasad

Alice Pritchard

Greg Pullman

Mollie Quasebarth

Katie & Steve Quinlivan

Julie & Mark Quinlivan

Yoshiko & Tony Quinlivan

Kish Rajan

Ann Randazzo

David Rattray

Suzanne Reed

Lisa Reimers

Mario Rendon

Nicole Rice

Kate Roberts

Sarah Rock

Mario Rodriguez

Raoul Rodriguez

Vy & Doug Rotenberg

Shawn Rohmiller

Dan Rounds

Fred Ruiz

Helen Rule

Martha Russell

Jessie Ryan

Nancy Ryan

Alma Salazar

Dan Salah

Alejandro Sandoval

Rob Sanger

Ken Sawyer

Martin Scaglione

Nathan Selzer

Michele Siqueiros

Martin Simon

Abdi Soltani

Gail Schoettler

Evan Schmidt

JD Schramm

Dan Schwartz

Jack Scott

Kurt Scott

Bill Scroggins

Celina Shands

Grant Shmelzer

Lynn Shaw

Valerie Shaw

Rona Sherriff

Vivian Shimoyama

Erik Skinner

Triana Silton

Monty Sullivan

Abby Snay

Sarah Speakman

Eboni Speight

Katie Spiker

Paul Steenhausen

Bettie Steiger

Bruce Stenslie

Rachael Stephens

Mitchell Stevens

Vincent Stewart

Jeff Strohl

Duf Sundheim	Dan Troy	Nicola & Paul Weiskopf
Dexter Suzuki	Rachel Unruh	Steve Westly
Sara Svirsky	Rob Urstein	Maureen White
Richard Swanson	Johan Uvin	Caroline Whistler
Ashley Swearingen	David Vliet	Lynell Wiggins
Tony Symonds	Ann Volk	Matt Williams
Theresa Tena	John Vu	Tracey Wills
Eric Thomas	Pham Vu	David Wolf
Patricia Thomas	Amy Wallace	Kevin & Lo Kim Woolley
Jim Thompson	Pam Walker	Jennifer Worth
James Timbie	Linda Wah	Julie Meier Wright
Thao Ton & Jason Burcombe	Peg Walton	Portia Wu
Mari & Andy Ton	Ruth Watkins	Warren Wu
David Toole	Pete Weber	Soo Ling Youngblood
Ricardo Torres	Micah Weinberg	Alan Zaremberg

Thank you also to my collaborators on this book: Salwa Emerson, Vanessa Mendozzi, Eric van der Hope, Nicholas Quinlivan, and Celeste & John Quinlivan.

About the Author

Van Ton-Quinlivan is a nationally recognized thought leader in workforce development and a catalyst for creating inclusive social and economic mobility for students through higher education. Her distinguished career spans the public, private, and nonprofit sectors.

Ton-Quinlivan served as executive vice chancellor of workforce and digital futures of the California Community Colleges and brought about significant public investment growth in career education. She has been quoted as an expert on higher education in the *New York Times, Chronicle of Higher Education, Insider Higher Education, Stanford Social Innovation Review, U.S. News & World Report,* and other publications. She is a frequent speaker at events hosted by the National Governors Association, Brookings Institute, Aspen Institute, Stanford's Hoover Institution, RAND

Corporation, and numerous other forums.

Currently, Ton-Quinlivan is the CEO of Futuro Health, whose nonprofit mission is to improve the health and wealth of communities by growing the largest network of credentialed allied healthcare workers in the nation.

In 2013, Ton-Quinlivan was named a White House Champion of Change under the Obama administration in recognition of her notable career in industry, education, and service as a community leader. She received the California Steward Leader Award in 2017 for her dedication to collaboration and work with public, private, and civic leaders to support economic and social mobility for state residents. Ton-Quinlivan was included in Sacramento magazine's 2018 "Powered by Women" list of leaders inspiring positive change. In 2019, she was named a mediaX distinguished visiting scholar by Stanford University.

Ton-Quinlivan earned her master's degrees from the Stanford Graduate School of Education and the Stanford Graduate School of Business and has an honorary doctorate from Golden Gate University. She serves on the boards of the National Skills Coalition, National Student Clearinghouse, and California Forward and advises the Putting America Back to Work venture fund.

Ton-Quinlivan resides in Northern California with her husband and two sons.

About Podcast

Stay current by listening to the
WorkforceRx with Futuro Health
podcast series
available on
Apple Podcast, Spotify, Google Podcast and more.
Or, visit futurohealth.org/podcast.

There has never been a stronger need for workers to adapt.
To keep up with the speed of change,
we must be prepared to shift into new jobs roles and pick up new skills.
Traditional approaches no longer suffice.
Van Ton-Quinlivan, in her role as Futuro Health CEO,
interviews leaders and innovators for insights into
the future of work, future of care, future of higher education,
and alternative education-to-work models.
We will need to draw on our collective ingenuity
to uncover ways to develop work, workers, and economic opportunity.

Index

Made in the USA
Columbia, SC
16 October 2021

47155145R00159